CONTENTS

CW00728240

1: THE MIND–BODY PROBLEM 1
Historical background 1
    The humours 2
    Descartes 2
    Dualism 3
The modern view 4
Biopsychology 5
Summary 5

2: EMOTION 6
What are emotions? 6
    Emotions and moods 6
    Are emotions universal? 7
    The physiological response 8
Theories of emotion 10
    Common sense 10
    The James–Lange theory 11
    The Cannon–Bard Theory 11
    Cognitive labelling theory 12
    Attention and attribution (a diversion) 14
    Attribution theory 14
    Cognitive appraisal theory 15
Summary 17

3: MOTIVATION 18
The concept of motivation 18
    Activity and behaviour 19
Theories of motivation 20
    Homeostasis 20
    Drive reduction theory 24
    Sexual drive 26
Social motives 28
Hierarchy of needs 28
Summary 30

4: STRESS AND THE BODY 31
Introduction to stress 31
    Stress meaning stressors 31
    Stress meaning strain 32
    Stress as an interaction 32
    Stress as change 35
The effects of stress on the body 35
    Psycho-neuro-immunology 36
The effect of stressors on the body 37
    Noise 37
    Temperature control 39
    Circadian rhythms 39
    Other sources of stress 41
Summary 42

5: STRESS, ILLNESS AND HEALTH 43
The relationship between stress and illness 43
Can stress have a direct effect on illness? 43
    Stressful events and the immune system 44
    Stress and respiratory illness 45
    Natural painkillers 45
Stress related to illness in vulnerable individuals 47
Stress, changes in behaviour, and illness 47
Relationship between social factors,
    psychology and biology 48
    Stress and heart disease 48
Reducing stress 50
    Coping strategies 50
Summary 52

Further Reading 53
References 53
Glossary 55
Acknowledgements 57
Answers to Self-Assessment Questions 58

The Mind–Body Problem

> KEY AIMS: By the end of Part 1 you will:
> ➤ be able to describe dualism;
> ➤ be able to discuss the influence of dualism on thinking today;
> ➤ be able to define bio-psychology.

SOMETHING TO TRY

Do we think of the body and mind as being different? Look up the standard dictionary definitions. You will find that there are many meanings for both terms, which only adds to the confusion when discussing the meanings in psychology.

The mind–body problem has challenged philosophers and scientists for generations and continues to do so. A book about the history of philosophy was recently written as a novel (*Sophie's World*), and has been a bestseller (Gaarder, 1995). Within psychology today there are still divisions between those who regard themselves as **psychophysiologists** and those who think of themselves as cognitive or social psychologists. Psychophysiologists study the interaction between physiology and behaviour, and cognitive psychologists study the interaction between thinking or problem-solving and behaviour. Health psychology and psychobiology attempt to integrate the two approaches, and to show that much behaviour results from interaction between the processes of mind and body.

Historical background

The ancient Greeks described reality as being made up of a physical world and a world of ideas. We know about the physical world because we can see, hear and feel it. Plato (c. 427–347 BC) suggested that reality has different levels:

- Our senses tell us about the real world, although they can be false and illusory. Cinema films or live television seem to be very real but they are actually only optical patterns.

Figure 1.1: Plato (c. 427–347 BC).

- True objects have physical properties and tend to be consistent. A chair has function and stability. When you go to sit down, you make assumptions that the chair will support you. In slapstick comedy, these assumptions are challenged, and if a chair collapses under someone, it is hard not to laugh.

- Science gives us laws about the relationship between objects which allow us to predict events.

- The world of pure ideas is at the highest level and this might include mathematical theory.

This view of the world led to **dualism.** Everything in the world has essential and physical qualities. Mind is firmly not of the physical world. If the mind and body are separate, theories of illness need to take account of this.

1

The humours

The humoral theory of illness was proposed by Hippocrates (c. 460–380 BC). The body contains four fluids (or **humours)** – blood, phlegm, yellow bile and black bile. If these are out of balance, people will get sick, and the type of illness will reflect the particular imbalance of different fluids. Hippocrates also suggested that personality was associated with a dominant fluid. Thus blood was associated with a sanguine personality, phlegm with being phlegmatic, yellow bile with a choleric temperament, and black bile with a melancholic personality. These have given us adjectives which we still use to describe personalities today.

However, this theory does not allow for any influence of the mind on the body's health, and it considers that the mind and body work independently. These ideas persisted well into the Middle Ages and beyond.

The belief that people had souls inhibited scientific research for many hundreds of years and dissection of humans was forbidden by the Church. Illness was thought to be caused by evil, and sickness was seen as God's punishment for wickedness. Even today, some people believe that AIDS has arisen as a punishment for promiscuity or homosexuality.

Descartes

There was a surge of thinking and a revival of science during the Renaissance era of the fourteenth and fifteenth centuries, but Rene Descartes (1596–1650), a seventeenth-century French philosopher, was the founder of today's scientific approach (Gross, 1996). He made three important advances:

Figure 1.2: René Descartes (1596–1650).

- He considered that the mind and body were separate, but suggested that living things could be understood by describing them carefully and by understanding the function of parts of the body. We can understand how the body works in the same way as we might understand how a clock works. We might take the clock to bits (anatomy) and observe how the wheels and cogs interact (physiology). However, we cannot find out anything about the clockmaker from analysing the clock, although we may speculate. The clock is not alive and has no **self-awareness.**

- Descartes did not believe that machines had souls, and the distinction between people, and other animals and inanimate objects, was that people had souls. At death the soul left the body. This meant that the body could be dissected.

- He also suggested that the mind and body could communicate. He thought that this was through the **pineal gland.** Later we shall see that the pineal gland was not the link, but other parts of the brain do link closely with the endocrine system, so Descartes had the right principle. We might wonder whether what we think of as 'the mind' is the same as what Descartes thought of as 'the soul'.

SAQ
1

How would you describe a character in a computer game to a contemporary of Descartes? Would you be able to say that it was alive in any way?

Figure 1.3: Reflex action as envisaged by Descartes. In this sketch by Descartes, the heat from the fire, A, starts a chain of processes that begins at the affected spot of the skin, B, and continues up the nerve tube until a pore of a cavity, F, is opened. Descartes believed that this opening allowed the animal spirits in the cavity to enter the nerve tube and eventually travel to the muscles which pull the foot from the fire. (From Descartes, 1662.)

This idea that the body was a machine (although inhabited by a soul) meant that behaviour could be explained in a mechanical way (see *Figure* 1.3). The modern day equivalent of automata or mechanical toys might be computer games. Automata mimicked the behaviour of humans in most elaborate ways, but they were not human because they were not living, and this challenged biologists to define what they meant by life.

SAQ
2

List what you would consider to be typical characteristics of living organisms.

The mechanistic approach of Descartes helps us to understand how our behaviour alters in response to external events. Stimuli are received through the senses and we can observe a reaction from the muscles (or **endocrine** or **immune systems**). There are connections between these which take place in the nervous system. A mechanistic approach is essential to understand the physiology of the body, but it does not give us the whole picture. As we shall see later in the discussion of hunger (p. 21), the central nervous system does more than just relay messages, or, in Descartes' terms, pull a thread.

Dualism
Dualism continued to be the prevailing view in science in the eighteenth and nineteenth century. Indeed, much current Western thinking is based on the work of philosophers. Two concepts in particular are important.

1   Complex systems or organisms are built up of simpler systems or organisms. If we understand a principle at one level, we can apply it to more complex levels. This is an important principle of biology, and applies equally to biopsychology. If we want to understand a complex system then it is useful to break it down into simpler systems. This is called **reductionism**.

2   The real world has a permanency in time and space. We cannot physically move through time and we cannot make objects move by the power of thought. In the unreal world of our mind we can do this. We can dream, we can fantasize, and in literature we can visit new worlds, different centuries and change race or gender. We distinguish between the real

3

world where the laws of physics hold, and the unreal world where these laws do not apply. In the real world everything has a cause and is determined.

Dualism has also been used to distinguish between the physical body and the spiritual. This makes for even more confusion between mind and soul.

A POSSIBLE PROJECT

Think of some science fiction or fantasy novels you have read, or films you have seen. Describe some rules that have been broken. For example, telepathy has not been proven scientifically, but if it were possible, the world might be a different place.

Another approach is **monism**, which says that either only mental events (**idealism**) are real, or that only physical events are real (**materialism**).

The modern view

Behaviour is part of the real world and subject to the same scientific laws as the physical body. The working of the body is not independent of thoughts, and so in order to understand how the body works we also need to know about thinking. It would be very difficult to regard thinking as part of a mind that was not part of the real world. **Interactionism** is dualism because it recognizes that mind and body are separate, but it suggests that the mind influences the body and the body influences the mind. If we take this approach, the question about whether or not there are two separate states becomes irrelevant. Advances in neuroscience have changed this view and say that thought process can be studied in the brain in the same way as we study changes in the composition of the blood.

In practice, life is even more complicated, because thought and emotions interact with our physical bodies, and with our life style. They all occupy the same conceptual space. When we consider the concept of stress (p. 31), we will discuss the biopsychosocial framework, and you will see how much we have moved on in the debate.

SAQ
3

What has philosophy got to do with a book on biopsychology?

The concept of dualism continues to be influential and the arguments can be likened to the nature (or genetics) versus environment debate. Some questions can't be answered because one cannot exist independently of the other. There is no evidence of a mind other than in an living body, and animal life, almost by definition, has a mind in the sense of a nervous system. Of course this does not tell us anything about plants or about the soul.

Biopsychology

'Pleasures, joys, laughter and jests as well as sorrows, pain, griefs and tears originate in the brain.' (Hippocrates)

Biological psychology is sometimes called biopsychology, and sometimes psychobiology, but whatever the name, it means the relationship of behaviour and thinking with physiology, including the nervous system, the endocrine system, and the immune system. An understanding of the brain is essential and this has been considered in a companion Unit in this series.

The investigation of biological mechanisms often requires very different techniques from those used in social psychology experiments or personality tests. These investigations may take place in the laboratory and understanding may come from laboratory experiments; these are described in most introductory textbooks. In this Unit we will look at the biological bases of motivation, emotion, and stress. Of course, there are also important social and cognitive aspects to these topics, and these should be borne in mind.

We will discuss the related themes of motivation and emotion in this Unit. Simplistic models are not adequate to explain complex human behaviour. Dualism is not useful in trying to understand either emotion or motivation. Our emotions are felt as a cognitive experience, and this experience is associated with physical changes in the body. Theories of motivation explain survival behaviour, but also need to explain higher order activities.

Stress is a broad term and may include aspects of life style, the reaction of our bodies and ways in which we cope with change. There is a link with illness, probably through the immune system, and we shall see that the stress–illness link is a good example of the application of the biopsychosocial approach.

Summary

1   Ideas about the relationship between the mind and the body have been influenced by the early Greeks and philosophers.

2   Descartes considered that the mind and body were separate, but that they could communicate, and that the soul left the body at death.

3   Dualism includes the concepts of reductionism, which is the explanation of a complex system by simpler systems, and a distinction between the real physical world and the unreal world of the mind.

4   The modern view is that behaviour is part of the real world and subject to the same scientific laws as the physical body.

Emotion

> KEY AIMS: By the end of Part 2 you will:
> ➤ be able to describe the physiological response to emotional arousal;
> ➤ be able to compare theories of emotion;
> ➤ be able to define relevant terms which are highlighted in bold.

What are emotions?

There have been many attempts to define **emotions.** Definitions depend on theories, as we will discover. A simple definition is that 'emotions are the experience of subjective feelings which have positive or negative value for the individual' (Stratton and Hayes, 1988). They can be usefully distinguished from states such as hunger, as feeling hungry is not accompanied by strong feelings of emotional arousal and may be very mild (at least to begin with). Emotions can also be distinguished from behaviour. If someone is running, they may be fleeing from a predator and feeling an emotion called fear. Another person who is running might be jogging for exercise, and they would have emotional feelings of achievement and satisfaction.

The term emotion can be used in many different ways, and 92 distinct definitions, organized into eleven separate categories, have been described in one paper (Kleinginna and Kleinginna, 1981). However, we can probably reduce this number.

SOMETHING TO TRY

List as many different emotions as you can. Emotions tend to share common characteristics and some of these characteristics are described below. How do the emotions in your list fit into these?

- A simple idea of emotion is that it is an individual experience that is *caused by something.* Emotions are intentional and focus on an object. You are proud or afraid *of* something. If you feel afraid in the absence of a recognizable object, this may be defined as **free floating anxiety** and indicate a pathological state; that is, 'I am worried, but I don't know why'.

- Emotions are *positive* or *negative*. We recognize excitement as positive but fear as negative.

- Emotions are usually *transitory.* They describe a short-lived change in our feelings. Grieving does not continue with the same intensity over a long period (and nor, I am afraid, does romantic love!).

Emotions and moods

Emotions differ from **moods.** Moods may not be caused by anything obvious, and someone may feel depressed for no apparent reason. Mood states last for relatively long periods of time.

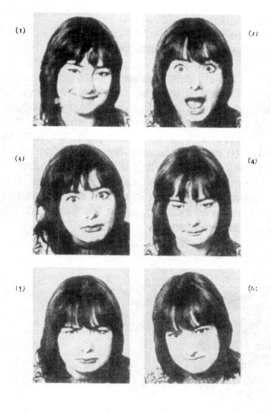

Figure 2.1: The six main facial expressions: (1) happiness; (2) surprise; (3) fear; (4) sadness; (5) anger; (6) disgust.

An emotional state may be described as an emotion in some circumstances, and a mood in others, so emotions and moods may not be distinct categories. Sadness may be a feeling of being low (mood), or may be felt in response to a loss (emotion). Categories of emotion are not distinct and this is known as a **prototype** approach. The category is defined by its most central and characteristic example, or prototype. The classical view of categories is that it is possible to give each emotion a tight and precise definition. Thus, there might be emotions described as happiness, fear, sadness, anger, surprise and disgust that are distinct from each other (Ekman, 1994). Some psychologists have suggested that emotions have their own facial expressions (see *Figure 2.1*). Darwin (1872) made careful observations of facial expressions in people and related these to emotions such as grief and laughter.

Are emotions universal?

If there are basic or primary emotions that are universal across cultures, then it can be argued that this is because they have adaptive value and have evolved through natural selection. If this is so, the contexts in which the emotions occur will have certain things in common. We would also expect to see them in other primates.

A POSSIBLE PROJECT

*Visit a zoo or watch a natural history programme on television. Can you recognize emotions in other animals? Some emotions such as fear are recognizable, although the facial expressions may be different, and sometimes may be observable in different ways. Ruffling of feathers, raising of crests or hair are responses to threat. We may be **anthropomorphic** in attributing emotions like pride or love to other animals, but we would probably agree that animals can feel pain.*

Parkinson (1995) argues that a common-sense view of emotions is that they have three levels:

- the individual (experience of emotion);
- the interpersonal (the expression of emotion); and
- the representational (ideas about emotion).

Researchers have tried to distinguish between between these three, but they may be very closely interlinked. If we want to study emotions we have to rely on our own experiences (which may be different from other people's), or alternatively we could study the expression of the emotion, whether this is by measuring physiological changes or by self report. **Cognitions**, or ideas of emotions, are not easy to put into words. The expression of emotions has a special place in art, possibly because it *is* difficult to put feelings into words. We try to express our emotions in many different ways, such as in poetry, or music, and we can recognize emotions in others through music or art. Think of a famous picture, such as Munch's painting *The Scream*, or how a particular piece of music reflects an emotion.

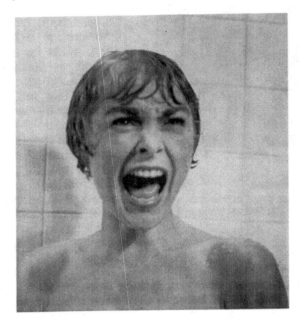

Figure 2.2: What emotion is being expressed here?

SOMETHING TO TRY

Rank the following terms in order of how well they represent your idea of an emotion: anger, hate, happiness, love, sadness.
Two hundred Canadian students ranked them in this order: love, hate, anger, happiness, sadness.
(Fehr and Russell, 1984)

The physiological response

Emotion can also be defined in terms of the physiological response. The experience of emotions is influenced by the activity of the **sympathetic nervous system** (SNS). In the SNS, *neurones* from the large nerve trunks run either side of the *spinal cord* and connect to organs of the body. There are subsequent changes in the body that accompany the emotional experience (see *Table 2.1*).

Table 2.1

What do you feel?	What is happening in the sympathetic nervous system?
heart racing and pounding	increased heart and blood pressure
mouth feels dry	saliva secretion suppressed
churning in stomach	stomach and intestines contract
no feeling of hunger	slows down peristalsis (the rhythmic waves of contractions in the smooth muscle of the digestive system)
sweat and hands feel clammy	increased sweating
loss of bladder control	sphincter muscles relax
rapid breathing	bronchi dilate pupils dilate glucose converted from glycogen

Nervous activity in the sympathetic nervous system stimulates the **adrenal glands** to secrete **adrenaline.** The adrenal glands lie on the dorsal side of the kidneys, and the adrenal medulla (see *Figure* 2.3) is activated by **preganglionic sympathetic axons.** A mixture of adrenaline (epinephrine) and *nor-adrenaline* (nor-epinephrine) is made by the chromaffin cells and released into the bloodstream. The effect on the body is to prepare the body for flight or fight (*Figure* 2.4).

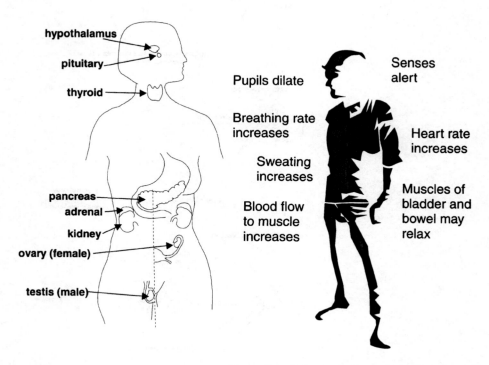

Figure 2.3: The endocrine glands.

Figure 2.4: Fight or flight – the effect on the sympathetic nervous system (SNS).

These hormones act as **neurotransmitters** for the sympathetic nervous system, and so enhance its activity. This is a loop. Activity in the sympathetic nervous system stimulates the adrenals, which produce the neurotransmitters adrenaline and nor-adrenaline, which themselves stimulate the sympathetic nerves.

Theories of emotion

Common sense

Common sense says that we experience emotion in response to stimuli, and then changes in our bodies and our behaviour occur (see *Figure 2.5a*). We feel happy when we watch a comedy show and laugh; we feel sad when we hear that someone has died and we may cry; and we feel apprehensive before a race and may sweat. However, we are sometimes aware that we only experience an emotion after the event. If you are skiing out of control and narrowly miss a tree, you may not feel frightened until you have stopped safely. The common-sense view of emotional reactions has been challenged by psychologists for the last 100 years.

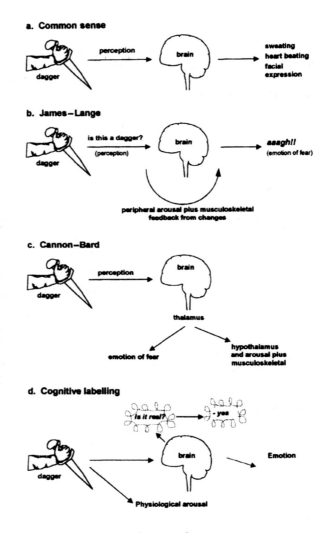

Figure 2.5: Theories of emotion.

Imagine you were asked to act the part of someone who has been left by their partner. You feel angry and sad. How would you convey these feelings to your audience?

You would probably change your behaviour in order to communicate your feelings. You would act differently, depending on how you were feeling. You might screw up your face, or mope, or stamp your foot. You might cry or swear. You would alter your outward behaviour but how would you feel inside?

Alternatively, you might think about the emotional aspects of the breakdown of the relationship, and these thoughts would lead to the natural expression of the emotions. This is sometimes known as 'method acting'.

The James–Lange theory

The **James–Lange theory** was proposed by the American psychologist, William James, in 1890, and also independently by a Danish physiologist, Carl Lange. It suggests that behaviour change leads to the experience of the emotion, which contrasts with the common-sense view. It implies that we do not hit because we are angry, but if we hit someone or something then we feel angry. According to this theory, if you saw a car approaching you at high speed as you crossed the road, you would first experience changes in the autonomic system such as your heart racing, and then, when the danger had passed, you would feel afraid (see *Figure 2.5b*).

> 'We feel sorry because we cry, angry because we strike, afraid because we tremble, and not that we cry, strike or tremble because we are sorry, angry or fearful, as the case may be.' (William James, 1890)

Of course, in everyday life we seek explanations for any physiological change. If symptoms such as sweaty hands, rapid heartbeat, and butterflies in the stomach occur without any apparent cause, they may indicate an acute anxiety state. We would worry if we experienced an emotion without any apparent cause. Other people might also worry about us, especially if it altered our behaviour. If someone became inexplicably angry we would find this disturbing. If they behaved aggressively, we might even be harmed.

SAQ 4

Anticipate a stressful event such as an exam, or making a difficult phone call. If you go over it in your mind (use mental rehearsal), you may find that your hands are sweating and your heart starts to pound. Does this support the James–Lange theory?

Think about a time in the past when you felt angry. Now tell someone about this while keeping your face smiling. Was it difficult to feel angry? Does this support the James–Lange theory?

The Cannon–Bard Theory

In the 1920s Walter Cannon and his student Philip Bard argued against the James–Lange theory. They pointed out that the same bodily responses occur in different arousal situations. The heart beats faster whether you are about to dive, running for a bus or escaping from a mugger. The subjective experience is quite different, therefore the cortical area of the brain *must* be involved.

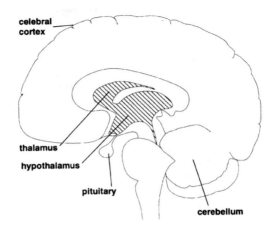

celebral cortex

thalamus

hypothalamus

pituitary

cerebellum

Figure 2.6: Cross-section of the brain.

The theory proposes that when something frightening is seen there are two effects on the brain, mediated by the thalamus (see *Figure 2.6*). An emotional state is experienced and the hypothalamus is activated, producing changes in the autonomic system. This means that our experience is not influenced by physiological activity, because the experience and the physiological changes occur at the same time (*Figure 2.5c*). In real life we feel emotions very quickly, but as the physiological response takes time, the responses cannot be the source of our emotions. This has been debated, and it has been found that some responses, such as increased heart rate, happen very quickly, whereas others, such as increased blood flow to the muscles, take longer.

The Cannon–Bard theory also suggests that the same response occurs in very different emotional states. Feeling ecstatically happy would be physiologically similar to feeling very angry. The psychological experience comes from the thalamus at the same time, or before, the physiological response.

Of course, there must be cognitive processing as well. The sight of an exam paper will have a different effect on a student who is well-prepared compared with the effect on one who has missed classes and has not revised. The Cannon–Bard theory does not explain why the social context matters.

 SOMETHING TO TRY

Imagine you have decided to go and see a film in which you know that there will be scenes of violence. Seeing a horrific car accident on a film is very different from seeing one in real life. Your responses may be similar but differ in degree, and the meaning of what you see is very different. You have probably chosen to see the film and paid money to do so. You expect that it will arouse your emotions, and might be disappointed if it did not. Your experience might depend on the company that you are in, and it might be different if you watched the film on video at home.

Why?

Consider your answer again after reading the section on motivation.

Cognitive labelling theory

This was proposed much later by Schachter and colleagues in the 1960s and is sometimes called the **cognitive theory of emotion.** This theory answered some of the problems about the cognitive and social contexts of arousal of emotion. It claimed that physiological changes do not cause emotion, as the James–Lange theory suggests, nor are psychological changes independent of physiological changes, as the Cannon–Bard theory suggests. Cognitive labelling theory suggests that physiological arousal is necessary for the experience of emotion, but it is how we interpret that meaning that matters (see *Figure 2.5d*). Physiological arousal is thus necessary for us to feel emotion, but the physiological change must also have meaning. We decide in a cognitive way whether the arousal is emotionally important (are we hot because of the room temperature or because we feel bothered and anxious?) and then we attribute an emotion to that state. Schachter and his colleagues carried out a series of experiments to test the theory (see *Box 2.1*).

Box 2.1: Cognitive labelling theory of emotion (Schachter and Singer, 1962)

Participants were told that they were to take part in an experiment on the effects of vitamins on vision. In fact, they were given an injection of either adrenaline or saline. They were divided into three experimental groups who were each given an injection of adrenaline, and one control group.

- Those in Group A were told about the real side effects of the injection of adrenaline.
- Those in Group B were given false information about the injection, such as it causing itching and headaches.
- Those in Group C were given no information about the effects of the injection.
- Group D was a control group and participants were given an injection of saline and no information about the effects.

They were then all asked to wait for the vision test. There was another person waiting with them, who, unknown to them, was a confederate of the experimenter. With half of the participants, the confederate acted in a euphoric way, laughing and playing with paper aeroplanes. With the other half he acted very angrily, eventually tearing up the questionnaire that they had been given to complete.

The behaviour of the participants in the four groups was assessed by an observer on the extent to which they joined in with the confederate's behaviour and by self reports.

Those in Group A who had had the real effects of the injection described to them, and Group D who had had no injection and no information given to them, were less likely to join in with the confederate and less likely to report feeling euphoric. Those in Group B who had been given false information about the effects of the injection, and those in Group C who had had the injection but no information were more likely to join in and to report euphoria.

How can we explain these results?

Group A experienced an emotional state and also had an explanation for it so they labelled their experience accordingly.

Group B and C had no information about what to expect and they labelled their experience based on what information they did have. This was what they assumed that the other person (unknown to them as a confederate) was experiencing.

Group D had no expectations, but they had no side effects (as they had only had a saline injection) and did not join in with the confederate.

However if the dose of adrenaline is high enough unpleasant reactions are found in all groups, so this may be a very sensitive response.

Attention and attribution (a diversion)

We saw in Part 1 that the relationship of brain and behaviour is complex. We try to make everyday sense of the messages that we get from the outside world and from our bodies. Normally (for example, as you are reading this), we are not aware of our bodies. However, you can change the focus of your attention. If I asked you to rate the present state of your body, you would think about the state of your muscles and might realize that, yes, you did have a somewhat aching back and, yes, your feet were cold, and, yes, you were aware of a slight headache. There has been no change in your body, but there has been a change in your cognition. You now feel an ache in your back and your hands feel cold, although nothing external has changed.

Pennebaker (1982) and colleagues carried out experiments on perception of symptoms. They showed that what we experience as symptoms depends on what we expect. In one experiment, one group was told that ultrasonic noise might cause an increase in skin temperature and another group that it might cause a decrease. They then listened to a blank tape that they had been told was ultrasonic noise. No changes were recorded in the skin temperature, but warmer or cooler warmer changes were reported depending whether they had been told to expect the temperature to rise or fall.

Attribution theory

This suggests that there are

- *internal* causes of behaviour (something to do with yourself); and
- *external* causes (to do with something in the environment or someone else).

You might then seek an explanation for your condition. Is your back aching because you had been picking strawberries the previous day? Is your head aching because you were drinking the night before? Are you feeling cold because the heating is on low? You seek to attribute the feeling to a cause. We seek causes of our own emotional state in the same way (we also seek causes for other people's behaviour). This is described as the **attribution** process and is usually considered in social psychology.

Weiner (1986) suggests that causes can be:

- internal or external (*locus dimension*);
- stable or unstable (*stability dimension*);
- controllable or uncontrollable (*controllability dimension*).

Consider these different reactions following a job interview:

1 You do badly in an interview and feel angry because the questions were difficult:

locus	external – the interview panel were hostile
stability	stable – it can't be changed
controllability	uncontrollable, outside your control

2   You do badly in the interview and feel disappointed because you had a bad cold coming on and did not do your best:

locus	internal – your body
stability	unstable – won't last
controllability	uncontrollable – can't help it

You do badly in the interview and feel depressed because you did not have the required abilities. Rate this on locus, stability and controllability dimensions.

The emotions that we feel (angry, disappointed or depressed) depend on our attribution of the causes. This is a very cognitive approach to emotion but might explain why people differ in their emotional responses. Some people get angry very easily and 'flare up'. This could be because they have a low threshold for physiological arousal, or it could be because their attributions are different.

You have to give a presentation to colleagues. As you wait your turn you become aware of your heart beating rapidly. How does cognitive labelling theory explain the two following scenarios?
1. You know that you will be graded on the quality of your presentation.
2. You are taking part in a rehabilitation programme following a heart attack.

Cognitive appraisal theory

Lazarus (1982) developed the cognitive labelling theory further (see *Figure* 2.7). He suggested that we experience emotion because of our appraisal of the situation. First, we evaluate the situation as being either positive, stressful or irrelevant to our well-being. This is known as **primary appraisal.** Then we consider the resources that we have for coping with the situation; this is **secondary appraisal**. Finally, we reappraise and monitor both the situation and our coping. This appraisal comes before any experience of emotion and it does not have to be conscious. This theory does not appear to take physiological changes into account. The study described in Box 2.2 illustrates how cognitions can affect emotional experience.

Zajonc (1984) argued that cognitions (ideas) and affect (mood state) operate under different systems. We may make very quick judgements about people with very little cognitive appraisal. We may not remember much about their physical appearance but we do remember what we felt about them. Some of these very quick responses may be more like reflexes than emotions. Gross (1996) suggests that if someone surprises you suddenly, you may show a startle response rather than a fear response. This could be described as very early appraisal.

The different theories of emotion may not be as conflicting as they may at first appear. Emotion can be elicited in the absence of cognition, but some cognitive processing is required for most emotion. Zajonc suggests that cognitions play a lesser role, but of course, some emotions like fear may occur very quickly while others, like love, may take longer, so giving more time for cognitive processing.

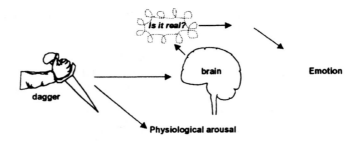

Figure 2.7: Cognitive appraisal.

Box 2.2: Cognitive appraisal theory

A famous study from the 1960s illustrates how cognitions can affect emotional experience (Speisman *et al.*, 1964).

An anthropological film was shown in which the penises of aboriginal boys were cut from tip to scrotum with a jagged knife. The context in which it was seen was manipulated.

- In condition 1 the group saw the film with no soundtrack (*silent control*).
- In condition 2 they heard a soundtrack in which the pain, danger and primitiveness of the operation were emphasized (*trauma*).
- In condition 3 the boys were shown as willing participants who looked forward to the happy conclusion of the ceremony as they entered manhood (*denial*).
- In condition 4 the emotional elements were ignored and the traditions of the tribe were stressed with a scientific narration accompanying the film (*intellectualization*).

The appraisal of stress was assessed by heart rate and galvanic skin response (GSR) during the film and self-report of the stress. The arousal was highest in group 2, the trauma group, followed by group 1, the silent control group, and then the denial and intellectualization groups. This suggests that emotional reaction is dependent on the primary appraisal of stress.

SAQ 7

Supposing someone got bad news, for example, that they had been made redundant. Their first reaction might be worry about loss of prestige and status. This might be followed by acute anxiety about money. These would be negative emotions. Alternatively, they might dislike their boss and take the opportunity to retrain and take another qualification. These would be positive emotions.

What secondary appraisal might follow? Contrast two outcomes — one that would lead to a positive outcome and one that would lead to negative outcome.

Table 2.2: Theories of emotion: the arguments

For	Against
Common-sense	
Simple and rational.	May experience the emotion after the event.
The James–Lange theory	
Changes in body are associated with changes in emotional experience.	Bodily changes are similar, so how do we know what emotions to experience in different situations?
We experience bodily changes before emotions.	Sometimes we experience emotions before the bodily changes.
Cannon–Bard theory	
The ANS responds to arousal in the same way.	It ignores cognitive components and the social context.
Cognitive labelling theory	
Cognitive aspects are considered. Whether the emotions are experienced and what we feel is determined by cognitive processes.	Arousal may not be pleasant. The experiments by Schachter are laboratory-based, and they have been difficult to replicate.
Cognitive appraisal	
Includes the social context. Agrees with daily experience.	Does not explain physiological changes.

Summary

1 Emotions have both physiological and psychological components.

2 We cannot account for actual experience without considering the social context, but equally physiological processes affect our emotional responses.

3 There is no one theory of emotion that is correct and they all have advantages and disadvantages (see Table 2.2).

Motivation

KEY AIMS: By the end of Part 3 you will:
➤ be able to describe theories of motivation;
➤ be able to discuss the concepts of hunger and thirst in relation to theory;
➤ be able to describe Maslow's hierarchy of needs as an example of the integration of physiology and psychology.

The concept of motivation

The concept of **motivation** has arisen because of the need to explain behaviour.

If I asked you why you got out of bed this morning there would be many possible explanations.

- A simple answer would be that the alarm went off. However, the ringing of the alarm is only a **stimulus** to behaviour. If you did not want to get up because it was the weekend, then you would not respond to the stimulus of the alarm.

A simple Stimulus–Response (S–R) relationship,

Stimulus (alarm) → Response (getting out of bed)

does not take into account motivation.

- Your bladder was full.

Again, this acted as a stimulus. The nervous impulses from the sphincter in the bladder reached the brain prompting the sphincter to be opened. The social conditioning that you acquired in childhood prevented emptying and eventually you woke up:

Stimulus (a full bladder) → Response (emptying).

The S–R connection is impeded by something going on in the brain. You get up to avoid wetting the bed and receiving social disapproval. Your own self-esteem might also be damaged as you could feel rather childlike if you wet the bed.

- You might be hungry or thirsty. There are physiological mechanisms that tell you that your body needs food or drink.

- You woke naturally and, although lying in bed was pleasant, there were more attractive things to do.

In this case, your need for sleep was satisfied, lying in bed was boring and you had other things to do. This might be study or a social activity. You might be more motivated to get up if the activity was important to you. The negative consequences of not getting up would also contribute to your motivation.

- It is automatic and I always get up in the morning.

This is known as a *learned habit*. You do it without thinking because this is what you always do. In this model motivation is less important. You might even get up automatically, realize that it was the weekend and go back to bed.

Activity and behaviour

Motivation impels activity. It can be defined as 'a general term given to an inferred underlying state which energises behaviour, causing it to take place' (Stratton and Hayes, 1988).

Motivated behaviour is behaviour that is directed towards a goal. It is behaviour with a purpose, but it would be hard to think of any behaviour that is *not* motivated. Even trivial behaviour, like playing computer games, must have some function, maybe entertainment or filling in time. In this sense, arguments become circular. If we do something, there must be a motive for doing it. Motives cause us to do something.

Psychologists seek to explain the causes of behaviour. As well as being of scientific interest, an understanding of the causal basis may help us to understand why things go wrong or behaviour becomes maladaptive. Understanding motives for eating may help us to treat obesity and anorexia nervosa (the 'slimming disease').

Why do we do anything at all? We obviously need to eat and drink to stay alive, but babies get fed without much effort on their part. As an infant matures it takes more control over its eating and drinking, and may even reject the food offered. By the time the child has grown into an adult, it regards the time of eating, type of food and quantity to be consumed to be a matter of personal choice. At the same time, there is a physiological mechanism that prompts people to eat. We may be able to explain the motivation of eating and drinking in physiological terms (see p. 21) but other behaviour is more difficult to explain.

- We all recognize the need for sleep and it can be a most powerful desire. Sometimes we experience great difficulty in resisting drowsiness. We probably feel we have more control over our intake of food than over our hours of sleep.

- We need stimulation and get bored if there is nothing to do. We also have social motives, for example, for the company of others, for affection and for achievement.

These may have a less obvious physiological basis, although there is evidence for a biological basis for pleasure. Attempts have been made to separate out physiological and non-physiological theories of motivation, but it is probably most useful to consider that they both interact.

If I asked you whether you eat because you are hungry, and you answered yes, I am sure that you could also think of some circumstances when:

1 you ate when you were not hungry; and
2 you were hungry but did not eat.

For example, we sometimes eat to keep someone company, or have another piece of cake out of politeness, or because we are very fond of chocolate. We might not eat when we are hungry when we want to lose weight, or when we are involved in an absorbing activity such as a rock climb, or fasting for religious reasons.

Theories of motivation

Just as we saw with theories of emotion, there are many different psychological theories and some are more closely related to physiology than others. William James (1890) described motivation in terms of instincts, and suggested that humans have social instincts as well as biological instincts. However, we need to postulate an awful lot of instincts to explain all human behaviour. Sigmund Freud (1914) proposed that there are two instincts or drives: a drive for life (**Eros**) and a death drive (**Thanatos**). These drives create psychic tension. Although Freud had a medical and biological background, he did not seek a biological explanation for his theories.

Homeostasis

This term describes the process whereby an organism maintains a steady state, for example, body temperature, blood sugar, salt concentration in the blood, and blood pressure (Cannon, 1932). If there is a change in the body, behaviour occurs to restore it to equilibrium. If you become too hot, there is an increase in blood flow to the body surface, and you sweat. This happens automatically and you do not have to decide to do anything. If the response is inadequate and you still feel hot, you may then remove some clothing or seek out some shade.

When the concept of homeostasis is applied to hunger, it is assumed that the physiology of the body works to maintain the body weight at some set point. The theory suggests that if food is scarce the metabolism will change so that the body becomes more efficient at using its reserves, and weight loss slows down.

SAQ 8

How does the concept of homeostasis explain why dieters find it difficult to lose weight?

The problems with the theory of homeostasis are:

- mammals such as rats and humans will eat more of a palatable (better tasting) food than an unpalatable one. Their eating pattern is not entirely regulated by their needs.
- it does not explain other needs, like sex and curiosity.
- the set point theory does not explain how the brain knows how fat the body is. A mechanism has yet to be identified, but it may involve **leptin**.
- it has been difficult to measure motivation without involving measurement of behaviour (see *Table 3.1*).

Table 3.1: Methods used to measure motivation in animal experiments

Measure of motivation	Method	Problem
amount consumed	weigh	reduces drive over time
unpalatable food	add bitter substance and measure persistence	depends on sensitivity of taste receptors
muscular activity	pull against a spring balance or speed of run towards food	depends on health of animal
level of electric shock accepted	animal must cross electric grid to reach food	may cause pain or injury
operant conditioning	rate of bar pressing in a Skinner box	depends on repertoire of animal

Most of these methods have been used on rats, which are the most often used experimental animals (with the exception of college students of psychology). Many of these methods would pose ethical questions if used today.

Homeostatic theories have been particularly applied to hunger and thirst and these will be considered in more detail.

Hunger

As you will have seen from your answer to the question on page 19, much of your eating behaviour is patterned into your daily life and not necessarily related to hunger. If you know that it is nearly lunchtime, you may feel hungry in anticipation.

Feeding very much depends on routines and habits – you do not always wait until you are hungry before eating. 'Comfort eating' or eating to satisfy emotional needs, may be an important cause of obesity (see *Figure* 3.1).

Figure 3.1: When faced with anxiety, Phyllis would always act promptly.

Similarly, hunger does not inevitably lead to eating, although there is clearly *some* relationship. When food has been eaten, the nutrients are absorbed from the intestine. Glucose is used for energy, and excess amino acids and glucose are stored in the form of glycogen in the muscles and adipose tissue. Fats are also stored in adipose tissue. Insulin, which is secreted by the pancreas, is needed for this conversion. After eating, the body uses energy derived from free fatty acids and glucose. However, brain cells use glucose, not free fatty acids.

The **glucostatic theory of hunger** (Mayer, 1955) suggests that hunger and satiety depend on the rate at which glucose is used in the body. Cells in the hypothalamus (see *Figure* 2.6, p. 12) monitor glucose levels. When the levels of glucose rise, satiety is signalled, and when they fall, hunger is signalled.

The difficulty with this simple and neat theory is that preloading (giving a high calorie food or drink) does not reliably reduce eating behaviour, and the variations in glucose supply to the brain are very small.

A protein called **leptin** was identified in 1994 and appears to control weight gain (Auwerx and Staels, 1998). High levels of leptin inform the brain that energy levels are sufficient, and low levels tell it that there are limited energy supplies. It also appears to have an effect on thyroid and adrenal steroid production.

There are other possible ways in which eating may be regulated (Kimble, 1988).

- There are glucose receptors in the liver and in the duodenum and they may play a part.

- It has been suggested that the hormone cholecystokinin (CCK), secreted in the small intestine, may suppress appetite.

- There may be a central control mechanism. Lesions in the ventral medial nucleus of the hypothalamus in rats cause overeating and eventual obesity (Stellar, 1954).

- In obese people more insulin is secreted in response to food cues. Increased insulin appears to increase appetite, probably by facilitating glucose entry into cells, lowering blood sugar and thereby increasing appetite.

Thirst

The simple **drive reduction theory** does not explain why we drink when we are not water deficient, and the **homeostatic theory** does not explain why we continue to drink. We usually drink because we like doing so. In psychological terms, we say that drinks have *positive* **incentive properties**. We anticipate the pleasurable effects of drinks. They may have pleasant tastes, like lemonade, or they may change our mood, like alcohol. The more we are deprived of water, the lower our threshold of positive value. If someone is deprived of water for a long period, they will drink the most unpalatable water.

The **double depletion theory** of thirst describes two sources of thirst. Changes in water content of both cellular fluid and extra-cellular fluid will influence thirst (Kimble, 1988).

Cellular fluid loss Most fluids are in the cells of the body. Antidiuretic hormone (ADH) is secreted by the pituitary (see *Figure* 2.6, p. 12). It acts on the kidneys to concentrate the urine to retain water in the body, and this conserves water. Experiments in rats have shown that when water is withdrawn from cells, rats drink more. If **hypertonic** solutions are injected into the hypothalamus they cause an increase in drinking (the cells shrink because water is lost through **osmosis**). If **hypotonic** solutions are injected they cause the cells to swell and drinking is reduced. Here we have a physiological mechanism in the hypothalamus which explains drinking behaviour.

Extra-cellular thirst This occurs when there is a loss of water from the fluids surrounding the cells of the body. This is known as *interstitial fluid* (between cells). After exercising and sweating the concentration of sodium ions (Na^+) and chlorine ions (Cl^-) increases in the blood plasma, and if it is more than about 0.9 per cent it is called **hypertonic**. Drinking water reduces the concentration to normal levels. The mechanisms are complex and involve changes in blood volume and enzyme release from the kidney.

Dry mouth theory The most obvious sign of thirst is a dry mouth. Walter Cannon suggested that as the salivary flow in the mouth decreases, we experience sensations of thirst and this triggers drinking. Perhaps this is why salted nuts are often offered with alcoholic drinks!

SAQ
9

To which theory of motivation considered so far does the dry mouth theory correspond?

However, it has been shown experimentally that dry mouth is not the only influence on thirst. In the 19th century, a French physiologist called Claude Bernard carried out sham drinking experiments on laboratory animals. This involved giving them water by mouth but not allowing it to be absorbed into the body. Openings, or fistulas, were made so that the water could escape. If the water reached the oesophagus and then left through a fistula, they had a wet mouth and throat, but they continued to drink. If water was placed directly into the dogs' stomachs, they stopped drinking (see *Figure* 3.2).

Problems with thirst as a unitary concept If thirst is a unitary motivational state, we should be able to predict the specific circumstances under which animals

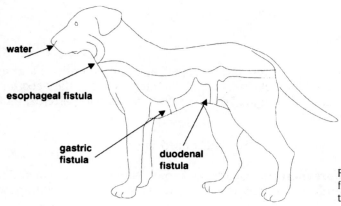

water

esophageal fistula

gastric
fistula

duodenal
fistula

Figure 3.2: The sites of fistulae in experiments in thirst.

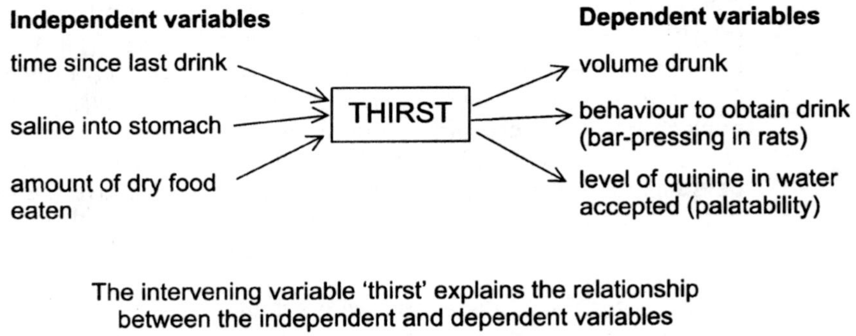

Figure 3.3: A model of thirst.

would drink. If an animal is deprived of water, or given saline into the stomach, or fed dry food, the theory says that it should experience thirst. To test the theory we would predict a change in behaviour. We still have to measure the effect of this motivational state on behaviour. There are a number of ways that have been used to measure thirst in animals (see Table 3.1, p. 21). If thirst is a simple unitary concept, then drinking behaviours would all change together. Manning and Dawkins (1995) describe experiments by physiologists which have measured thirst in rats by volume of water drunk, the rate at which a bar in a **Skinner Box** is pressed and level of quinine (a bitter tasting substance) accepted in water. The different measures of drinking did not always rise together, as would be expected if thirst were a single entity (see *Figure* 3.3).

Drive reduction theory

The definition of motivation as a state that energizes behaviour suggests that there is an internal process that impels us to satisfy some need. We experience this internal process as a feeling of hunger or a desire for someone's company. The felt need (sometimes called a **drive)** builds up until it prompts goal-seeking behaviour. The behaviour continues until the goals are reached. When the goal is reached, the need is satisfied and the goal-seeking behaviour ceases (see *Figure* 3.4).

Need → drive → goal-seeking behaviour → goal → drive reduction

Figure 3.4: Drive reduction

Needs may be independent of drives, and can be defined and measured. We can measure blood glucose levels which tell us about the need for food. Drives are concepts that underlie observable behaviour patterns, but cannot be measured directly.

Needs or motives can be categorized into:

- **primary motives** (sometimes known as biological or survival motives); and
- **secondary motives** (social or acquired motives which are learned).

Primary motives are considered to be *innate* and Hull (1943) identified the following:

- hunger, thirst, the need for air
- need to avoid injury
- need to maintain optimum temperature
- need to defecate and urinate
- need for rest or sleep
- need for activity
- need to reproduce

These are common to all mammals. Hull claimed that all behaviour originates in the satisfaction of these needs and these needs motivate through drives. Hull suggested that behaviour depends on the strength of the drive, together with learned habits or behaviour. However hungry a new-born kitten is, it cannot hunt for food.

If the goal of a primary drive is reached and the drive is reduced, this has a reinforcing effect. This is an underlying principle of learning theory. Any behaviour that results in the goal being achieved is more likely to occur again. This was described as operant conditioning by B. F. Skinner (1904–1990), who was one of the most influential American psychologists.

Secondary drives are acquired by **conditioning.** Drives for money, status, possession are acquired, but they can be just as motivating as primary drives.

SOMETHING TO TRY

Look at advertisements in magazines. How many attempt to promote a product by referring to primary motives (such as hunger or thirst) and how many by referring to secondary motives (status, power)?

There are problems with Hull's theory:

- The relationship of primary drives to needs is not simple. You may need company, but not all the time, and your drive will vary in intensity. Some goals are very desirable and have what is called incentive value. You may be driven to seek out and buy a bar of chocolate although you have no physiological need for a sugary, high fat food. Chocolate has a high incentive value and so activates a drive in the absence of need.

- Many incentives are socially determined. Winning a race is an incentive but it is difficult to argue that we have a need for the trophy.

- We may have needs that are not reflected in recognizable drives. We need a balanced diet but we do not experience a drive for fibre. Pleasure centres have been identified in the rat brain and electrical stimulation in these areas acts as a reinforcer. This suggests a neural mechanism that is unrelated to physiological state.

- Early experiments with rats (Tolman, 1948) have shown that learning can take place in the absence of drive reduction (**latent learning**).

- Hull's theory concentrated on primary drives, whereas much of human behaviour is dependent on secondary drives.

Sexual drive

The explanations of motivation of other drives are just as complex.

Sexual activity is not necessary for the survival of the individual but it is essential for the survival of the species. Dawkins (1976) discusses the evolution of behaviour and suggests that selection acts on our genes. Any behaviour that ensures the survival of our genes, whether carried by us or members of our family, will have adaptive value. Any behaviour that makes it more likely that genes will be passed on will have a selective advantage. For instance, it is in the interest of the male mammal to impregnate as many females as possible (providing that he establishes that they will make good mothers), while it is in the interest of the female to be more selective. She must ensure that any male that fertilizes her eggs carries genes that are likely to contribute to the survival of the offspring and so ensure the survival of her genes. Males and females are therefore likely to have different patterns of sexual behaviour. Of course, these are not conscious processes, but those individuals who carry genes for these behaviour patterns will be more likely to leave more offspring, and hence their genes will be more likely to spread in a population.

Sex is thus a non-homeostatic drive. It is useful to distinguish between *sexual arousal* and *sexual appetite* (Bancroft, 1989). Sexual arousal may be considered to be a drive like hunger, while sexual appetite is like feeling hungry. We feel hungrier the longer we are without food, and may want sexual activity more if we have been without it. We also learn to want food and to eat in certain circumstances. Sexual activity often takes place in certain places (in bed), at certain times (at night), and with certain people (partners). Of course, we are not bound by these restrictions and to some extent we can eat or have sex at any time and place. (However, there are *some* social restrictions on both activities.)

We experience a sexual appetite which stimulates us to seek sexual stimulation. This can come from the external environment, such as sights or smells, but it can also come from inner fantasies. Touch is a very powerful stimulus and can lead to further enhancement of sexual arousal and increased sexual appetite. The internal state (which corresponds to the glucostatic mechanisms in hunger) may be determined by hormones or by the biochemical state of the brain. In a highly aroused state, there may be a sexual response (for example, erection or orgasm) to minimal stimuli.

Sexual desire or appetite results from a complex interaction between cognitive processes, neurophysiological mechanisms and mood state.

- For sexual activity to take place, some cognitive process is necessary. People have to learn (and usually do so very rapidly) what it is that they find arousing.

- Recognition of sexual excitement may be pleasurable, but it can also result in fear, depending on the previous experiences of the person.

- The neurophysiological mechanisms underlying sexuality are very complex and, for obvious reasons, are difficult to study in humans.

- A depressed mood may lead to low sexual arousal. Loss of libido is recognized as a symptom of clinical depression. On the other hand positive mood or happiness may increase the chance of enjoyable sex, and enjoyable sex may make someone very happy.

The extent of control over sexual behaviour by hormones in primates depends on the social organization of the species. In experiments in sub-primate mammals, such as mice and rats, it has been found that sexual behaviour in the male disappears after castration. However, there is considerable variation in behaviour. Some animals appear to be more dependent on the level of male hormones (androgens) than others. In one experiment we observed a castrated male mouse that continued to copulate twice a week for over three months. We called him Mighty Mouse!

There are wide variations in sexual receptivity in female mammals. In many species, the female is only receptive at certain times. These may be regulated by the oestrous cycle. In some species, for example, deer, the female will only ovulate at certain times of the year; in others, such as badgers, ovulation is stimulated by copulation; and in others, for example, mice, ovulation occurs every three or four days. Unusually in the animal kingdom, sexual activity in humans occurs throughout the year. In women, sexual interest may be related to the time of the menstrual cycle, but the relationship is complex (see Box 3.1). Social and cognitive factors are closely involved in sexual activity in humans, but mating in some primate species is very much influenced by social structure (Manning and Dawkins, 1998).

Androgen levels appear to affect sexuality in men to some extent. Studies of hypogonadal men (having absent or impaired secondary sexual characteristics) have shown that replacement of androgens can restore sexual interest (Bancroft, 1989).

Box 3.1: The relationship between sexual interest and menstrual cycle

In a study of sexual activity through the menstrual cycle (Sanders et al., 1983), a significant peak in sexual activity was found after the menstrual period (the post-menstrual phase) compared with the late follicular or the peri ovulatory phase, when conception would be most likely. Sexual interest was linked to general mood and energy. Women who felt better in the middle third of the cycle were more likely to report sexual feelings at that time. When the effect of mood on sexual feelings was controlled, it appeared that there were peaks in the post-menstrual phase and in the pre-menstrual phase.

Why might women's moods change throughout the cycle, and affect their sexual interest? There may be central nervous system effects, but it is possible to give a social explanation. The pre-menstrual peak could have occurred because the women knew that they were likely to have a menstrual bleed the following week. They might have wanted to have more sex in anticipation of a week abstaining from sexual intercourse while bleeding. The post-menstrual peak could also be related to the preceding week's abstinence.

Social motives

There are other non-homeostatic motives, for example stimulus needs, curiosity, exploration and play.

Most mammals appear to have drives for exploration, manipulation and curiosity. If rats are put into a maze they will explore it even though there is no intrinsic reward. We would do the same in a new place. We may set out to see a specific tourist sight or simply wander around to get the feel of the place. Manipulative drive is also seen in animals. In a classic study, monkeys were given mechanical wire puzzles made up of interlocking metal pins, hooks and clasps (Butler and Harlow, 1954). They learned to solve the puzzles and continued to play with them without any external reward (see *Figure* 3.5).

Figure 3.5: The monkeys in this classic study learnt to solve mechanical wire puzzles.

Play is seen in many animals and in all primates. Play does not fulfil homeostatic needs or survival needs, but is seen particularly in young animals and probably has a learning function, although children find play intrinsically satisfying. You do not need to reward a child for playing, and children are unaware that play might have purpose. Play does lead to gradual acquisition of skills or of competence and it might be that mastery over the environment is motivating.

Hierarchy of needs

An attempt to integrate biological and psychological motivation was made by Abraham Maslow in the 1950s (Maslow, 1954). He suggested that there are:

- forces that ensure survival by satisfying physical and psychological needs. These are described as deficiency or D, motives, and are a means to an end.
- forces that promote self-actualization or the realization of one's full potential. These are exclusive to humans and not shared with other primates. They are described as being or B, motives, and are intrinsically satisfying.

These forces, motives or needs can be organized into a hierarchy in the shape of a pyramid (see *Figure* 3.6). A broad base of biological needs (D motives) progresses through security and safety needs, then aesthetic (artistic needs) and culminates in a peak of intellectual needs (B motives). The pyramid has the following properties:

- the lower layer of needs have to be satisfied before the next layer can be addressed;

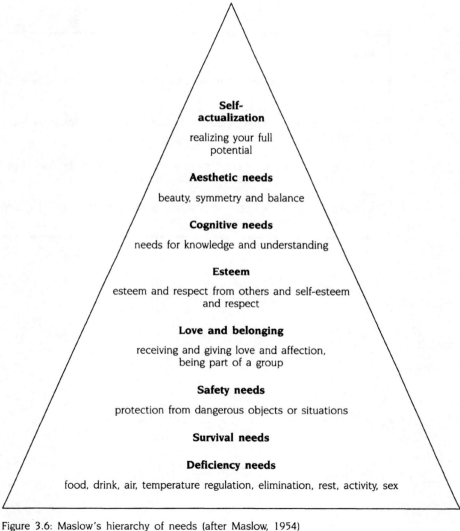

Self-actualization

realizing your full potential

Aesthetic needs

beauty, symmetry and balance

Cognitive needs

needs for knowledge and understanding

Esteem

esteem and respect from others and self-esteem and respect

Love and belonging

receiving and giving love and affection, being part of a group

Safety needs

protection from dangerous objects or situations

Survival needs

Deficiency needs

food, drink, air, temperature regulation, elimination, rest, activity, sex

Figure 3.6: Maslow's hierarchy of needs (after Maslow, 1954)

- higher level needs are a later evolutionary development;
- higher levels develop later in the life of the individual;
- the higher up the pyramid you go, the less biological the need becomes;
- the higher up the pyramid you go, the harder it becomes to satisfy the needs.

Problems with this theory are that:

- the hierarchy is a very general description and may not apply to individuals, and may not apply across different age groups, gender or races;
- needs at lower levels can be ignored if the higher one becomes more important. For example, in war soldiers may ignore safety; the scientist Marie Curie was so absorbed in her research that she forgot to eat;
- unconscious processes are ignored;
- those who reach the peak may be better educated and intelligent, and it may be very culture dependent;
- there is little experimental evidence to support Maslow's theory although it has been very popular in the healthcare professions and has **intuitive validity**.

Summary

1 Motivation is a complex topic, and there is unlikely to be one all-embracing theory.

2 The theories all have different attributes, and some may be more useful for describing some drives but not relevant to others.

3 Hunger may be controlled by glucose receptors in the liver and duodenum but also by central control mechanisms.

4 Sexual drive is a non-homeostatic drive and influenced by biological and cultural factors.

Stress and the Body

KEY AIMS: By the end of Part 4 you will:
➤ be able to distinguish between three different meanings of stress;
➤ be able to describe the **General Adaptation Syndrome** (GAS);
➤ be able to describe the essentials of the immune system;
➤ be able to discuss the effects of specific stressors.

Introduction to stress

The term 'stress' is most often used as a general term, meaning disagreeable stimuli, but it can have at least three meanings. These meanings tend to be confused, and stress is thought to precede a great variety of life's problems and ill health.

The terms **stress**, **stressor**, and **strain** all have precise meanings in mechanical engineering and physiology, but are often confused in psychology.

Stress meaning stressors

The term *stress* can be used to mean the stimuli that produce physiological, behavioural, and psychological responses to stress. These are usefully described as *stressors*. These are events that happen to a person that threaten or disturb, and may be further divided into the following categories.

- *Disasters* may be brief in time but may have long-lasting effects. The sinking of the pleasure cruiser the *Marchioness* in 1989 took a very short period of time, but it was followed by lasting psychological disturbances among survivors. Fifty-one people who were attending a birthday party died when the cruiser was hit by a 1500 ton dredger. A study of 27 survivors found significant psychological distress. The event was sudden; one moment they were celebrating with friends and minutes later they were in the cold, dark river. Many lost friends and suffered days of uncertainty before all the bodies were recovered (Thompson *et al.*, 1994).

- *Personal stressors* tend to be acute but have long-lasting effects. Life events (such as divorce, moving house) may be very disruptive, but they are likely to be infrequent. Some events will be predictable but it is those that are uncontrollable which are seen as most stressful.

- *Background stressors* are chronic and may include environmental factors such as noise, heat and overcrowding. Minor stressors or hassles may occur daily and are irritating. Losing something, being late, or an unexpected slight can all act as stressors, and their effect may add up to have an effect on health.

 SOMETHING TO TRY

Look through a copy of a newspaper. How many reports are about stressors? Can you classify them according to the categories just mentioned? What does this tell you about society today?

Change in itself may be stressful. Life events are events that cause significant change. They can be either positive or negative, but they all demand adjustment to new circumstances. Life events appear to precede a number of physical and psychological health problems, triggering or exacerbating psychological disorders and may lead to clinical anxiety or depression.

In the 1960s, Holmes and Rahe developed a scale to measure the impact of life events. They asked a group of people from the general population to rate the amount of adjustment that each life event would require. They identified 43 items and constructed a schedule of recent experiences (SRE), allocating a maximum of 100 life change units to death of a spouse. The total score of the scale was regarded as a measure of the degree of stress. The scales have been updated (Miller and Rahe, 1997) and the ranks in 1995 are compared with the original 1965 scale (see Box 4.1). You will see that there has been an increase in life stress since 1965.

There may not be a clear and direct relationship between life events and health. The life events may be related to each other, and many of these life events are not discrete events, so one major life event can have an effect on several of the other events all at once. Some of the relationships between life events and health may occur because of psychiatric disturbances following the event.

Stress meaning strain

The term 'stress' can also be taken to mean the *strain* or the physiological response to an event or stimulus. This is the meaning used by Hans Selye (1956) a Canadian endocrinologist. He distinguished between **distress** and **eustress:**

- *distress* is commonly used to mean negative effects of strain (from Greek *dys* meaning poor);
- *eustress* means the positive effects (from Greek *eu* meaning good).

Stress as an interaction

Stress can also be regarded as an interaction between the stimulus and the individual. Lazarus (1982) considered that the meaning of the event affected the reaction to it. The same event may not be seen as equally stressful by everyone.

Primary appraisal is the first reaction to an event, followed by secondary appraisal, and as the stressful event gets underway, there may be a reappraisal (see *Table* 4.1). The event may be seen as having been better (or worse) than had been expected, or it may be followed by relief that it is over.

Examinations are predictable stressful events that may be familiar to you. They will be stressful if you are ill-prepared or if the questions are unexpectedly difficult to answer. If the examinations include questions that had been anticipated and are straightforward, what had been seen as a stressful event may be reappraised as an enjoyable experience. (Of course, if the examination turned out to be worse than had been expected, it may be reappraised as a very negative and stressful experience).

Box 4.1: Social readjustment rating scale: Life changes scaling for the 1990s. (Based on Miller and Rahe, 1997.)

Rank	Life event	Life change units 1965	1995
1	death of spouse	100	119
2	divorce	73	98
3	marital separation	65	79
4	jail term	63	75
5	death of close family member	63	92
6	personal injury or illness	53	77
7	marriage	50	50
8	fired at work	47	79
9	marital reconciliation	45	57
10	retirement	45	54
11	change in health in family member	44	56
12	pregnancy	40	66
13	sex difficulties	39	45
14	gain of new family member	39	57
15	business readjustment	39	62
16	change in financial state	38	56
17	death of close friend	37	70
18	change to line of different work	36	51
19	change in number of arguments with spouse	35	51
20	mortgage over $10,000	31	44
21	foreclosure of mortgage or loan	30	61
22	change in responsibilities at work	29	43
23	son or daughter leaving home	29	44
24	trouble with in-laws	29	38
25	outstanding personal achievement	28	37
26	spouse begins or stops work	26	46
27	begin or end school	25	38
28	change in living conditions	24	42
29	revision of personal habits	23	27
30	trouble with boss	20	29
31	change in work hours or conditions	20	36
32	change in residence	20	41
33	change in schools	19	35
34	change in recreation	19	29
35	change in church activities	19	22
36	change in social activities	18	27
37	mortgage or loan less than $10,000	17	28
38	change in sleeping habits	16	26
39	change in number of family get-togethers	15	26
40	change in eating habits	15	27
41	vacation	13	25
42	Christmas	12	30
43	minor violations of the law	11	22
	Grand mean LCU values	**34**	**49**

Table 4.1: Possible stressful effects of being physically assaulted

Reaction	Immediate	Delayed
Emotional	fear or anxiety pain	depression
Physiological	release of adrenaline and nor-adrenaline increased heart rate and respiratory rate	reduced immune function
Cognitive effects	heightened arousal	lack of concentration flashbacks poor memory
Behavioural	fight or run	fear of people work absenteeism disturbed sleep

Some stress is desirable. Some people who have 'hardy' personalities (Kobasa, 1982) enjoy stress, and most of us know what it is like to be bored. We also need to be stimulated.

SAQ 10

Would you describe the strain of studying as eustress or distress?

We suggested in Part 3 that seeking simulation is a drive. Most animals will explore a new environment. Hebb (1966) suggested that individuals have an optimum level of stimulation and that we have ways of maintaining this. We strive to obtain a balance between boredom and over-stimulation. Zuckerman *et al.* (1978) devised a *Sensation Seeking Scale* (SSS). High scorers agreed with statements such as 'I would like to try new foods that I have never tasted before', and 'I can't stand watching a movie that I've seen before'. High scorers tend to be extrovert and independent and to value change and stimulation, and they are also more likely to smoke.

We often put ourselves in situations of stress and enjoy being stressed. Emotions such as fear can be aroused, but are only enjoyable because they are in a safe situation which is under control. One difference between watching a horror video and being in a real live situation may be the degree of control. The television can be turned off and you can close your eyes. We may be aware that it is fiction, not reality, although we are receiving stressful stimuli. Even so, it is surprising how long the stressful effects of fiction can last.

SOMETHING TO TRY

Recall the last disturbing film or programme you saw. If you watched it late at night, did you dream about it? Can you recall it now? What were the stressful factors?

Stress as change

Look back at the discussion of homeostasis on p. 20. Change is a disruption of normal predictable events. A stressor is a challenge or a threat to normal physiological processes (like a poison) or to lifestyle (like moving house) or to psychological functioning (like the ending, or beginning, of a relationship).

The amount of stress may depend on the extent of the change. A small change in the weather is not a stressor but a heatwave is.

People are constantly adjusting to change in both physiological and psychological terms. Some people adapt to change easily and others find it much harder. Elderly people sometimes resist change and take longer to adapt to new living conditions or to loss. It is interesting that their bodies also have poorer homeostatic mechanisms.

SAQ
11

What implications does the concept of homeostasis have in practice?

What might happen to an elderly person if there was a cold spell? Would a young person be affected in the same way?

The effects of stress on the body

We can't separate out the physical effects on the body from the psychological effects because of the way the body and mind interact (see Part 1). *Table* 4.1 shows how a stressful event can have many effects.

We have seen that with heightened arousal the autonomic nervous system is stimulated and the adrenal medulla releases adrenaline into the bloodstream. This happens relatively quickly. If the arousal is prolonged then there is a further reaction.

The hypothalamus stimulates the pituitary gland which is anatomically close to it at the base of the brain (see *Figure* 2.6). Two hormones are produced which affect the body's reaction. Thyrotrophic hormone (TTH) stimulates the thyroid gland which makes more energy available to the body. Adreno-cortico-trophic hormone (ACTH) stimulates the adrenal cortex (see *Figure* 2.3). This causes the release of many cortico steroids. These include the glucocorticosteroids which control the amount of glucose in the blood.

If chronic stress persists, the adrenals enlarge. Animals may become ill and die. For example, males of a small carnivorous marsupial called *Antechinus stuartii* live for just under a year and all die over a three-week period following mating. During mating there is a great deal of aggression between the males, which is likely to alter the metabolism of the adrenals. However, if the males are kept in cages on their own they live well over a year (Lee *et al.*, 1977, cited in Manning and Dawkins, 1998).

ACTH also has a negative effect on the immune system. It depresses the ability of natural killer cells to destroy cancer cells.

Hans Selye published an influential book on stress and the reaction of the body (Selye, 1956). He suggested that stress was a non-specific response that could occur as a result of many different stressors. The organism tries to adapt to change and restore the equilibrium of homeostasis. The general adaptive response to nonspecific stimuli was described as a **General Adaptation Syndrome** (GAS). This has three stages:

- alarm reaction
- stage of resistance
- stage of exhaustion

At the first alarm, adrenaline (from the adrenal medulla, see Part 2) is produced. If the stressful situation persists, the organism enters the stage of resistance and ACTH is produced. This initially protects, but if it is prolonged there are negative effects, such as the effect on the immune system. If there is chronic stress, the stimulation of the adrenals by the pituitary hormones continues and the control of glucose levels is disrupted.

This is a description of the physiological process (stress as strain) and does not tell us about the stressful experience.

There are problems with the GAS theory:

- the model was derived from the results of animal experiments and so cognitive and emotional factors were probably underestimated. In real life, stressors that produce the felt experience of stress tend to be emotional. Having a painful injection is not the same as having an unexpected class test, although both could be considered stressful.
- the role of non-specific factors is over-emphasized.
- stressors do not all produce the same changes in hormone levels.

Psycho-neuro-immunology

Selye had suggested that stressors could affect the immune system (see Box 4.1) and this was one mechanism that caused the stage of exhaustion. The immune system plays an important part in the effects of stress on the body and, as we shall see in Part 5, on health and illness (Lovallo, 1997).

The immune system enables the animal to recognize foreign bodies (for example, bacteria, viruses) or their own abnormal cells (known as antigens), to neutralize them and then recognize them again.

Stress can affect the immune system in four ways:

1 cytokines, produced by the immune system cells, stimulate the central nervous system;
2 the central nervous system regulates the immune response through the pituitary adreno cortical axis;
3 immune system cells have receptors for adrenaline;
4 lymphoid tissues are connected by neurones to the ANS.

Stress can reduce immune system functions. When corticosteroid levels are raised and the sympathetic nervous system is activated, the immune response is suppressed. We will return to a discussion of the effect of immune suppression on disease in Part 5.

The effect of stressors on the body

Noise

Noise is unwanted sound. One person's heavy metal music might be another
person's nightmare (see *Figure* 4.1).

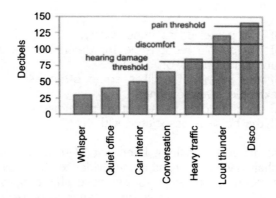

Figure 4.1: The effects of noise levels on hearing.

 SOMETHING TO TRY

*What kinds of noise do you find stressful? Is it loud noise, or intermittent noise? Does the
context – disco or library – matter? Would it be different if you had a headache? Does it
matter if you can't control it? Is the association, for example, an ambulance siren,
important? Is unexpected noise stressful?*

*If you can't think of a stressful noisy event, try blowing up a balloon until it bursts (no
responsibility taken for this suggestion!).*

The effect of chronic noise can be screened out by focusing out the noise. We
can do this quite effectively. At a party you can concentrate on what one

person is saying while other people are talking around you. You do not attend to the rest of the conversations going on around you unless someone says your name. You may be able to listen to two conversations at once, particularly if you are bored, and this is known as the **cocktail party phenomonon** (Cherry, 1953).

A POSSIBLE PROJECT

Tape record a party or a conversation with friends. You will hear all sorts of background noises which you were unaware of at the time. I once taped an entire research interview underneath a budgie cage. The replies were lost under budgie chirping, although I had been completely unaware of this at the time!

Intense noise increases physiological arousal and increases the release of adrenaline. There are physiological effects of adrenaline (see p. 9).

What effect would a loud sudden noise have on the body?

The loudness (greater intensity) of the noise will affect how stressful it is (Hygge, 1997) but other factors may also cause noise to be regarded as stressful, such as:

- if it is perceived as unnecessary;
- if the people responsible for the noise are though to be unconcerned about its effects on others;
- if the individual dislikes some other aspects of the environment (for example, overcrowding);
- if the individual believes that the noise is harmful to health;
- if the noise is associated with fear.

Noise at work has long been regarded as a source of stress (Cooper and Marshall, 1978). There is some evidence that noise levels above 80 decibels on a recurring prolonged basis cause physiological stress. However, it is less stressful if it is predictable and change in noise levels is more stressful than absolute levels (Sutherland and Cooper, 1990). Whether or not there is a physiological effect, noise is disliked and perceived as stressful. Noise was found to be a significant predictor of job dissatisfaction among workers on drilling rigs and platforms in the North Sea. It may increase vulnerability to accidents. Exposure to noise is associated with reported fatigue, headaches, irritability and poor concentration. It may also affect interpersonal relations at work.

Noise can also affect hearing. Temporary threshold shifts (changes in the level of noise that can be detected) occur at about 70 decibels for bands about 4 kHz, and around 75 decibels for bands around 250 Hz if presented for several hours. Noise above 75 decibels may carry a risk of hearing impairment. If there is prolonged exposure without any rest in between, there may be irreversible damage to the hair cells of the ear, and permanent hearing impairment.

Ask a sample of young adults about their exposure to disco music and any effects they felt on their hearing after going to a concert or club. Then ask a sample of older people about noise levels that they find stressful. Does either group perceive any effect on their hearing or on their health? Why might young people be able to tolerate very loud noise levels that older people would find intolerable?

Temperature control

How do you feel when you are very hot? Would it be different if you were lying on a beach or listening to a lecture? The context in which we experience temperature change, and our expectations of it it will affect our reaction. Just as in the case of noise, unpredictable change in temperature is more stressful than predictable change.

In the USA, violence in cities is much more likely in the hot summer months. Some people feel irritable when it is hot and elderly people find it hard to cope with temperature extremes. This may be because their temperature control is poor or because they find it difficult to cope with change.

Studies have shown that work demanding critical decisions, fine discrimination and performance of fast or skilled action tends to be performed less well in either hot or cold conditions. People tend to be more stressed by overheated working conditions than by the cold.

Circadian rhythms

Change is stressful, and a change in our daily routines may be stressful because it disrupts our regular pattern of living. Humans as well as other animals have rhythms of activity. These are called **circadian rhythms** (from the Latin *circa dies*, 'about a day'). Every 24 hours there are cycles of heart rate, metabolic rate, hormone production and body temperature.

The rhythms are not exactly 24 hours long. If we deprive animals of external cues to day length (free running), their waking time gradually shifts. Normally the 24 hour clock is reset every day by external cues called **zeitgebers** (the German for 'time givers'). These cues are normally changes in light and dark.

We are usually unaware of these cycles, although we are aware of our sleep rhythms.

Sleep

Sleep is a periodic state of unconsciousness, which lasts about eight hours a day in most people. Sleep can be studied by observing people in sleep laboratories using an electro encephalograph (EEG). Electrodes are placed on the scalp and record the brain waves. During each night's sleep we move through different depths of sleep (Empsom, 1989), passing from an alpha wave pattern (8–12 cycles per second), into a theta pattern (3–7 cycles per second), and then into a delta pattern (½ to 1 cycles per second) or slow wave sleep (SWS) (see *Figure* 4.2). In the delta pattern we experience deep sleep. Every 90 minutes or so we have a burst of activity with rapid eye movement (REM), accompanied by physiological changes such as increased blood flow, heart rate and respiration rate. Dreaming is associated with REM sleep but may continue throughout the night. We go through this cycle about four times in a night, and as the night progresses we spend more and time in REM sleep. If we are deprived of sleep there is a rebound effect and we have more REM sleep when we catch up.

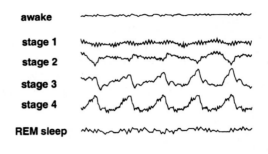

Figure 4.2: Brain wave patterns during sleep.

You might ask how we know that the recordings made on people with wires attached to their heads and sleeping in a university research laboratory are sleeping in the same way that they would do at home. Studies on healthy young adults participating in laboratory experiments have shown that on the first night it is difficult for them to get to sleep and they show more time in light sleep. On the second and subsequent night there is no change, and experiments in sleep laboratories begin after one night's acclimatization. Think how on holiday you often find that the first night in a strange bed is less restful, but you soon get used to it.

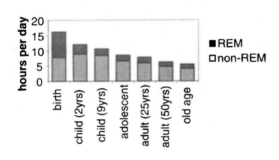

Figure 4.3: Changes in REM sleep with age.

Babies spend a great deal of their time asleep, with the time spent asleep getting less with increasing age (see *Figure* 4.3). The relative time spent at different levels also changes. Elderly people appear to need less SWS, and if they nap during the day, they may find it harder to maintain sleep during the night.

Is disrupted sleep stressful?

If the brain is stimulated, for example by studying late at night, there is increased cortical activity, and any worry or anxiety you may be experiencing can make sleep difficult. Night shift workers find that they can fall asleep quite quickly during the day but wake up a few hours later. This is because their other physiological rhythms are tuned into a different cycle. They may then drop off during the day, increasing the risk of accidents. In spite of feeling worse after losing sleep, people are surprisingly capable of compensating. Reaction times are not necessarily slowed down, possibly because people make an extra effort to keep awake. It is thought that one effect of sleep loss is to increase the number of *microsleeps*, or lapses in attention. There appear to be individual differences in that some people can adapt more quickly than others to sleep disruption.

You might wonder if it is possible to sleep too much. One way of coping with a stressful situation is to withdraw from it (see Part 5). We do this very effectively by sleeping, but of course this does not solve the problem. Experiments on extending sleep or displacing sleep found that performance on some mental tasks was reduced.

It is not easy to shift sleeping patterns. It is much more difficult to go to sleep earlier (**phase advance**) and get up earlier, than to go to sleep four hours later and get up later (**phase delay**). Most people suffer much less from jet lag when travelling from East to West than from West to East. This may be because an increase in day length is easier to deal with than a decrease.

SAQ 13

Does travelling from Washington to London involve a phase advance or phase delay?

Other sources of stress
Some working conditions have specific stressors

Vibration
Vibration is a source of stress resulting in nausea, loss of balance, and fatigue. The use of pneumatic drills can affect hands and feet, as well as ears.

Sick building syndrome
Sick building syndrome refers to the observation that some buildings are not designed for the people that work in them. Most people spend most of their adult waking life at work, and prefer to see daylight, and to be able to communicate with fellow workers. If the working conditions are poor and perceived as stressful, there may be adverse consequences for health and productivity.

Figure 4.4: Urban living is accompanied by many stressors.

New technology

New technology may be stressful. If the work environment changes rapidly, skills may become obsolete. Workers are expected to learn new skills and, as we have seen, changes are often stressors. Changes in organization, changes in the use of computers, and changes in management style may all be perceived as stressful. These changes are not likely to produce an acute stress response, but the effects of stress may build up gradually. Urban living (see Figure 4.4) brings with it many stressors, such as noise, traffic, crowding and a fast pace of life. Living in the country may be considered as being less stressful, but there may be stresses there too because of social isolation, greater poverty, and limited opportunities for work or education.

Change

Although change may be stressful, *lack* of change may be just as bad. Sutherland and Cooper (1990) describe studies that have investigated stress in factory workers. Work on an assembly line can be boring and give no feeling of achievement or satisfaction, and in one study, electronic assemblers had a high frequency of micro sleeps.

SAQ 14

What kind of stress reaction would you expect to find in people working in dangerous occupations such as fire fighters or prison officers?

Summary

1 Stress can have three very different meanings: stressors, strain, and stress as an interaction.

2 Stress affects the body because of effects on the autonomic nervous system and on the immune system.

3 Four models have been used to explain the effects of stress on illness; a direct effect, stress causing illness in vulnerable individuals, stress leading to changes in behaviour causing illness and the social context influencing the relationship between stress and illness.

4 Approaches to reducing stress depend on the definition and may be problem-centred or symptom-centred.

Stress, Illness and Health

KEY AIMS: By the end of Part 5 you will:
➤ be able to describe the relationship between stress and illness;
➤ be able to describe the effects of illness on stress;
➤ be able to distinguish between emotion-centred and problem-centred methods of reducing stress.

The relationship between stress and illness

Stress may be a cause of illness, and being ill can itself be stressful. People who are chronically ill may feel pain, discomfort and depression – we might describe them as being *stressed*. However, able-bodied people are sometimes surprised at how well those with impairment or disabilities cope. The amputation of a leg may appear to one person to be highly stressful, but another person may accept and tolerate it, especially if it means that there is less pain.

The results of animal research suggest that there is a physiological effect of stress. Lazarus's approach suggests that stress (strain) results from the failure to cope. This gives us a relationship between the failure to cope and physical illness. The most likely mechanism is *physiological change*.

If someone had been described to you as being 'run down' or 'under the weather', you might expect them to be more likely to become ill. You would probably include illness of the body, as well as mental illnesses.

Psychologists have taken different approaches to understanding the relationships between stress and illness. As we have seen before, they often use models to make sense of the observation that stressful events are associated with illness (Lovallo, 1997). Four models have been suggested, and we will now look at these.

1 Stress ───────────→ **illness**

2 Stress ───────────→ **illness in vulnerable individuals**

3 Stress ───────────→ **changes in behaviour** ───────→ **illness**

4 Social context, ──────→ **stress** ─────────────────→ **illness**
  psychology and biology

Figure 5.1: Models of stress and health or illness.

Can stress have a direct effect on illness?

When people are ill they try to find the cause of their illness. This process is known as **attribution** and in the same way that we try to explain the cause of our feelings, we also try to explain the causes of our illnesses. The most usual medical model is that of the germ model (see *Figure 5.2*). The cause may be bacteria or viruses (or even **prions**). The biological mechanisms are not always understood, even with the germ model. Many people ask their doctors for antibiotic therapy for viral infections such as influenza, even though it is only effective for bacterial infections.

Bug ⟶ the immune system ⟶ + ⟶ illness
⟶ − ⟶ health

Figure 5.2. The germ model of illness.

However, not all illness can be explained by a simple germ theory because not everyone gets ill if they are exposed to a virus. Some people seem to be more vulnerable than others. We are aware that there are differences in resistance to illness, and this knowledge may enter our attribution. Perhaps someone gets ill after eating raw egg because they are vulnerable due to a previous illness or because they are pregnant, or because they are very old or very young. There is then a small step to the conclusion that some people get ill because they have low resistance, and that this might be an effect of stress.

The biological explanation for this difference in vulnerability could lie in the immune system (see p. 36). The effect of stress on the immune system has been studied by health psychologists and psychobiologists (Bachen et al., 1997). The immune system, the central nervous system and the endocrine system are all interrelated. The immune system controls production of lymphocytes and antibodies. The lymphocytes include T helper cells, T killer cells and T stressor cells which influence antibody production (see Box 4.2). Any change in lymphocyte production will affect the response to illness.

Stressful events and the immune system

After the damage to the Three Mile Island (TMI) nuclear reactor in the USA in 1979, it was found that there was more distress and higher latent antibody levels in TMI residents compared to controls more than six years later (McKinnon et al., 1989). The residents also had lower levels of lymphocytes and NK cells.

An almost universal and predictable time of stress in normal health adults is when they take academic examinations. Studies of medical students by Kiecolt-Glaser and colleagues (Kiecolt-Glaser et al.,1984) showed that there was a decrease in the number of T cells, reduced NK cell activity, increased plasma levels of circulating antibodies and decreased cytokine production before and during major exams compared with test-free periods.

It is difficult to anticipate most stressful events (apart from exams and childbirth!), so there have been attempts to carry out laboratory experiments on the effects of stress on the immune system (Bachen et al., 1997). After acute stress, such as a loud burst of noise, NK cell activity rises and then returns to baseline a short time later. However, in real life, stressors usually last longer. In chronic stress, levels of NK cells and T suppresser/cytotoxic lymphocytes tend to increase. The changes in the immune system are complex and may also be affected by changes in cortisol levels.

The relationship between immune activity and disease is not straightforward either. It might be thought that the more immune activity the better, but although this might lead to the reduction of risk of disease, it might also increase the risk of **auto immune disease**.

Stress and respiratory illness

Evans and Edgerton (1991) measured 52 minor life events from daily diaries kept by a hundred clerical workers. The minor events were classified as either 'uplifts', which are positive events like receiving a letter or being praised, or 'hassles' which are negative events like losing something or being stuck in traffic. The clerical workers also rated their physical health and mood state. Events in the four days before the onset of a cold were compared with the previous three days in the same week. The scores of 'uplifts' were significantly fewer and there was a trend for greater 'hassles'. The most important hassles were those which concerned not meeting self-expectations or failures of intentions. The most important significant uplifts were having close interactions with spouse or partner.

Figure 5.3: A positive event, such as being complimented or having a conversation with a good friend, is termed an 'uplift'.

However, in a recent replication, Stone *et al.* (1993) assessed 79 middle-aged men and followed them for twelve weeks. They used the same methodology as the studies by Evans and Edgerton, but found no differences in the ratings of desirable events (uplifts), or undesirable events in days preceding illness.

In trying to understand the differences between the result of the studies of Evans and Edgerton and the studies of Stone we find that there are differences in their definitions of illness. People vary in their illness behaviour and symptom reporting. The links between illness and reporting are not clear, but it seems likely that if someone is feeling low than their behaviour will change. If they have a mild infection then they may feel low and focus on their symptoms, so the interactions are complex.

Natural painkillers

It is reported that soldiers on the battlefield do not report pain immediately after they have been injured, but that the pain comes later. It has been suggested that the production of **endogenous opioid peptides** helps to cope with the pain. In the 1970s opiate receptors were found in animal brains. Kosterlitz and colleagues at Aberdeen University, Scotland, then identified two endogenous opiates, winning the Nobel Prize for their research. Eventually five

Figure 5.4: Runner's high – an example of eustress?

peptides were discovered, often known as **endorphins**, or the body's natural painkillers.

It is difficult to measure the production of endorphins because it involves taking samples of cerebro spinal fluid. An alternative experimental approach has been adopted. *Stimulation Produced Anaesthesia* (SPA) is the reduction in sensitivity to pain produced by electrical simulation of the brain in unanaesthetized animals or people. SPA can be eliminated by small concentrations of naxolone. It can therefore be concluded that an endogenous opioid system has caused pain relief. There is some evidence that this is so, but pain relief is a complex issue (Horn and Munafo, 1997).

After strenuous exercise (which may be physically stressful but psychologically relaxing) some people report elated mood and feelings of euphoria. This might be because of a release of endorphins. Endorphin release may also deaden muscle pain from muscle fatigue. Naxolone has again been used to see if it could reverse the effect. **Double blind studies,** where neither the subject nor the experimenter (nor those carrying out the assays) know which group has had the active substance and which has had the placebo, are essential in this kind of research (see *Box 5.1*).

Box 5.1: Methodology of research.

When we find conflicting results it is important to look closely at the differences in the methodology of the research. If you continue with your studies in psychology you will find a critical appraisal approach very useful in assessing evidence (Crombie, 1996). There is a move towards evidence-based medicine where clinical practice is based on a review of the evidence. There is so much information and research published about health and illness (and stress) that it is impossible for clinicians or psychologists to keep up with all the research in more than a few areas.

Randomized controlled trials are the soundest kind of evidence to be considered in critical appraisal. Evidence-based reviews are used to identify research which is rigorous and it is hoped that these reviews will then inform clinical practice.

Major events such as the damage to the nuclear reactor at Three Mile Island may also affect health by changing the levels of cortisol secreted by the adrenal cortex (see *Figure* 2.3). Schaeffer and Baum (1984) found that residents in the Three Mile Island area had higher levels of self-reported physical and mental symptoms compared with control subjects.

Stress related to illness in vulnerable individuals

As we have seen, the meaning of the stressful event may be important in determining a person's reaction. Some people may be stress-prone. They see life's hassles as more intense and are then more likely to become ill (Levy and Heiden, 1991).

It is not easy to find good evidence for a relationship between psychological vulnerability and physical illness. If we find that people suffering from an illness (the cases) differ from those without the illness, but are similar in other ways (the controls), we might think that the differences caused the illness. However, this does not tell us about causality and the difference may result from the diagnosis rather than from factors causing the illness. People who have been given a diagnosis may later think of themselves as being 'ill'.

A diagnosis of a malignant breast tumour is likely to be a stressful event for anybody. Greer and Morris (1978) assessed 160 consecutive patients admitted for breast tumour biopsies. Forty per cent of the biopsies were malignant. Five years later they assessed the survival rate and found that those that had shown either 'denial' or 'a fighting spirit' had a better survival rate than those who showed 'stoic acceptance' or 'helpless/hopelessness'. However, the effect of the attitude towards the disease may depend on what stage the diagnosis is made as well as on the stage of the disease. It is likely that we have many potential cancers in our bodies and that these are dealt with by the immune system. Early cancers are therefore more likely to be affected by psychological factors influencing the immune system. Factors such as extroversion, depression and stressful life events were not significantly related to the progress of the breast cancer. These findings suggest that coming to terms with an illness may not necessarily be beneficial.

Of course, there might be some factors that influence both the attitude and the illness, or there might be a direct effect of the attitude on the progress of the illness. Social factors may alter immune function. Apart from nutritional factors that might affect health it has also been shown that long term unemployment is linked to poor immunological functioning (Arnetz, 1987).

Stress, changes in behaviour, and illness

What do people do when they are stressed? Could any behaviour that might help to reduce the symptoms of stress do more harm than good?

- When people are feeling stressed they may eat more high calorie foods such as chocolate (which can be very comforting). This may disturb the sympathetic nervous system or endocrine system and have a direct physiological effect.

- People may drink more alcohol when they are stressed. Alcohol consumption is directly related to raised blood pressure levels. Blood pressure falls if alcohol intake is reduced.

- Smoking may increase. Cigarette smoking is one of the major influences on cardiovascular and respiratory illness.

- A stressful event may trigger a behaviour change. Someone who is widowed may lose weight and this could be a direct effect of stress on metabolism. It could be because the person loses their appetite. It could also be because it is difficult cooking for one and less enjoyable eating alone.

SAQ 15

Some ways of coping with stress may benefit health. Can you think of any?

Relaxation training has been shown to be effective in reducing systolic and diastolic blood pressure levels. The effect of relaxation programmes could come from the relaxation itself, but it was noted in many studies that groups receiving relaxation programmes also showed other changes in general health and an increase in life satisfaction. Relaxation has been shown to be effective in reducing self-reported pain (Linton, 1982). Relaxation decreases autonomic arousal and skeletal muscle tension and increases peripheral blood flow.

SAQ 16

Why is it difficult to carry out a double blind randomized controlled trial of relaxation therapy?

Relationship between social factors, psychology and biology

In the Introduction to this Unit (p. 5) we discussed the value of a biopsychosocial approach. This approach is well-illustrated in considering pre-menstrual syndrome (PMS) and chronic fatigue syndrome (CFS, formerly called ME) and is described in Box 5.2.

Cardiac disease is one of the major causes of death in the western world and its recent increase has been related to the stress of modern society. It has been extensively studied by health psychologists, and it is closely related to health behaviour (Carroll, 1992).

Stress and heart disease

The risk of heart disease may be associated with a stressful lifestyle. Two cardiologists in the USA, Freidman and Rosenman, observed that many of their cardiac patients could be characterized as being highly competitive, ambitious, impatient, and aggressive. They described this as being Type A. Type B were those who did not show these characteristics.

To see if these characteristics predicted heart disease, they carried out a major research study known as *The Western Collaborative Group Study*. They assessed and followed up over 3000 men (aged 39–59) for eight and a half years. Those that had been described as Type A were twice as likely than Type B to have had a heart attack (Rosenmann *et al.*, 1975). In another large study in California, both men and women were assessed, and Type A assessment again predicted heart attacks (Haynes *et al.*, 1980). Attempts to relate the Type A behaviour pattern to the physiology of cardiac disease have produced conflicting results (Kop and Krantz, 1997). The relationship may not be as clear as first appeared. When factors such as cholesterol levels, blood pressure and body weight were controlled, the results were not replicated. The differences may be in the measurement of Type A, or selection of people who were at high risk into the study. Type A is more usefully seen as a general behaviour pattern rather than a personality trait, and can be modified.

The four models of stress and illness can be well illustrated by looking at skin problems. At one time, skin diseases were thought to be related to personality and there are clinical reports of a high incidence of psychiatric problems in skin clinics (James, 1995).

Relate each of the following statements to the four models of stress discussed.

A.   *In certain types or conditions of skin (for example, an inflammation) scratching will make it worse. The eventual skin problem could be related to the behaviour.*

B.   *The problem is caused by the behaviour of scratching. Eczema can cause severe itching that makes the sufferer want to scratch. If they do, it will make it worse, but if they resist they may feel frustrated, leading to physiological stress that could also make it worse.*

C.   *Some individuals may be more prone to the problem, have a lower level of personal control and react badly to it, thereby becoming more stressed.*

D.   *Changes in blood flow or skin conductivity have direct effects on skin condition.*

Box 5.2: Pre-menstrual syndrome (PMS) and chronic fatigue syndrome (CFS).

A number of studies report negative changes in the pre-menstrual week, and in particular they have found increases in fluid retention, breast tenderness and irritability. This has been called pre-menstrual syndrome (PMS). In a study of premenstrual changes, 138 student nurses kept diaries of their general health (Slade, 1984). Both male and female students kept diaries and the purpose of the study was kept hidden from them. Complete data were obtained from 118 participants and the symptoms were related to the time of onset of menstruation. There were peaks in scores for pain and water retention in the pre-menstrual and menstrual phases but not for concentration, behavioural changes or negative affect. PMS sufferers may attribute negative symptoms to hormonal changes and they may see them as being under external control. The time of the menstrual cycle may be relevant even if there is no biological relationship. Even though we do not understand the mechanism, if the woman herself perceives a change, then this could influence her illness behaviour.

Chronic fatigue syndrome (CFS) may be diagnosed in someone with no identifiable organic disease who persistently complains of fatigue, and it has often been linked to stress. In a qualitative study it was found that many sufferers believed that their illness had been caused by an infection and that stress played a part (Clements et al., 1997). They believed that they could partially control the *symptoms* by reducing activity but felt helpless to control the *physical disease process*. Coping with symptoms often included limiting exercise, avoiding certain foods, and doing anything to avoid 'stress'. Both PMS and CFS are complex issues and may be the result of a combination of biological and psychological factors.

Reducing stress

A POSSIBLE PROJECT

Look for articles on newspapers and magazines that discuss the topic of stress in relation to health. You may find stress included in discussions about work, vitamin supplements or relationships.

As I write, there is a television cartoon in the UK featuring a character called Eric who caricatures the stress encountered in every day life. How do fictional characters in literature and soaps cope with life? To what extent are plots dependent on the failure to cope?

Reduction of stress depends on the definition of stress. If stress is a stressor or stressful event, it might be possible to change it in a practical way. If stress is strain and expressed as anxiety, then a symptom-focused approach such as relaxation might reduce it. Lazarus and Folkman (1984) proposed that coping with stress could be either *problem-centred* or *emotion-centred*.

In a problem-centred approach, efforts are directed at managing or alleviating the stressful situation. Problem-solving approaches may be more appropriate for moderate levels of stress that are potentially long-term, but capable of change, for example, work situations or chronic illness. A stressful situation such as a feud with neighbours could be solved by moving house, a personality clash at work could be solved by changing jobs. Stress in an academic course could be solved by dropping out, but of course this may result in a new set of stressors.

The problem-focused strategy need not be practical. The feud with the neighbours might be resolved by arbitration by a third party. The personality clash might be resolved by a reassessment of roles with the help of a counsellor.

SAQ
18

Think of problem-focused ways to reduce the stress of an academic course.

Often these solutions are not practicable (or even desirable) so in emotion-centred coping people try to control their reaction to the stress.

Emotion-centred problem-solving can be used to maintain hope and keep up spirits. This might be important in coping with bereavement or coping with high levels of stress such as war or life-threatening situations.

Coping strategies

Antonovsky (1979) describes three components of coping strategies:

* *Rationality*
  This is the accurate objective assessment of the stressful situation. It is difficult to see how there can be an objective assessment of a stressor. However, there may be some agreement on the relative stressfulness of an event.

- *Flexibility*

  There are usually a number of different possible ways of dealing with a stressful situation, and the ability to consider a range is a useful coping strategy.

- *Farsightedness*

  This means thinking through the consequences. This is often helped by discussing the problem with someone else.

Help from others?

Social support has been shown to have a beneficial effect on mental health. However, in many studies it was not clear whether it was the actual social support received (often measured in terms of the number of contacts with others) or the perceived social support (whether the person felt that they were getting the attention that they should). Caspi (1987) measured hassles, social support and mood. Mood scores were less affected by the previous day's hassles if the participants had more perceived social support. This suggests that minor stresses will be more easily borne if the person feels they are emotionally supported. It is interesting to observe how much better people feel when they have talked about their worry and received reassurance or sympathy.

SOMETHING TO TRY

How might the theory of social support explain the ease with which some people tell their life stories to 'strangers on the train'? Have you ever been in this situation? Ask your friends and family for their experiences.

Social support may reduce the stress response and so have a positive physiological effect. This protective effect of social support is sometimes described as **buffering**. Social support might provide a buffer against the effects of stress. Ganster and Victor (1988) reviewed a large number of studies and suggested that there might be many different factors that could explain the buffering effect. Social support may change the behaviour of people. People on their own may adopt different eating patterns from people living in families. An elderly person may be more likely to put on the heating if there is someone else to share it, and in general may take more care over their health and appearance for the sake of the other family members. Social support probably boosts self-esteem, and as we see ourselves through the responses of others, their perception of our health will affect our self-perception.

Biofeedback

Biofeedback is the perception of the results of some biological activity. We get feedback all the time in real life. If you close your eyes you know that you are sitting upright because of the messages from your muscles and the semicircular canals in your ears. You may also remember that that is what you were doing when you had your eyes open and you haven't moved since.

We use biofeedback to learn how to acquire new motor skills. In learning to ride a bicycle, we get continuous feedback from our perception of our balance and progress along the road.

This is conscious, but there are also unconscious biofeedback mechanisms operating all the time in our bodies. You are not aware of your pulse unless you deliberately measure it, but it is being monitored at an unconscious level.

The term 'biofeedback' is often used to mean a technique for monitoring some physiological activity and converting it into an auditory or visual message (Gatchel, 1997). It has been shown that tension headaches and heart rate can be controlled by giving feedback without any external reward. It seems that the feedback and the consequent perceived control are intrinsically rewarding. There have been many attempts to use biofeedback to manage stress, but its impact on treatment of disease has been disputed (Gatchel, 1997).

Stress control by anxiolytic drugs

Stress is sometimes experienced as anxiety. The symptoms of anxiety include rapid breathing, palpitations and 'butterflies in the stomach' and these can be controlled by drug therapy. Benzodiazapines, such as Valium (diazepam) and Librium were taken by large numbers of people in the 1970s, often for many years. These tranquillizers are effective in reducing the symptoms of anxiety, but also have side effects such as drowsiness and negative effects on learning, attention and memory. They are used to treat free floating anxiety. This is where the person is anxious in general, not just in anticipation of a stressor like an exam. They are used less now, partly because of fears of dependence.

The physical effects of anxiety, such as palpitations, or sweating, are more likely to be controlled by β-adrenoceptor blockers such as propanolol, known as beta-blockers. They block peripheral sympathetic activity.

SAQ 19

Which kind of drug would be most effective in controlling symptoms of rapid breathing in response to stress, the benzodiazapines or the beta-blockers?

Summary

1 The immune system may be the link between the experience of stress and subsequent illness.

2 Some people may be more vulnerable to the effects of stress.

3 People may change their behaviour when stressed, so increasing the risk of illness.

4 Heart disease has been associated with behaviour known as Type A.

5 Focusing on problems or symptoms, adopting coping strategies, social support, biofeedback and anxiolytic drugs can reduce stress.

FURTHER READING

Gross, R. (1996). *Psychology: The science of mind and behaviour, 3rd edn.* London: Hodder and Stoughton. This is an introductory textbook primarily written for pre-degree students. Part II is a comprehensive account of the biological basis of behaviour.

Sarafino, E.P. (1998). *Health Psychology: Biopsychosocial interactions, 3rd edn.* Chichester: John Wiley. This is one of many health psychology textbooks. It has a particular emphasis on biological aspects, and Part II has three chapters on stress.

Kimble, D.P. (1992). *Biological Psychology.* London: Harcourt, Brace, Jovanovich. An undergraduate text which gives extensive biological background.

Lovallo, W.R. (1997). *Stress and Health: Biological and psychological interactions.* Thousand Oaks, CA: Sage. A very readable up-to-date paperback with an excellent discussion of the mind/body debate.

REFERENCES

Antonovsky, A. (1979). *Health, Stress and Coping.* San Francisco, CA: Jossey-Bass.

Arnetz, B.B., Wasserman, J., Petrini, B., Brenner, A.O., Levi, L., Eneroth, P., Salovaara, H., Hjelm, R., Salovaara, L., Theorell, T., and Petterson, I.L. (1987). Immune function in unemployed women. *Psychosomatic Medicine,* 49, 3–12.

Auwerx, J. and Staels, B. (1998). Leptin. *The Lancet,* 351, 737–742.

Bachen, E., Cohen, S., Marsland, A.L. (1997). Psychoimmunology. In A. Baum, S. Newman, J. Weinman, R. West, and C. McManus (Eds) *Cambridge Handbook of Psychology, Health and Medicine.* Cambridge: Cambridge University Press.

Bancroft, J. (1989). *Human Sexuality and Its Problems, 2nd edn.* Edinburgh: Churchill Livingstone.

Butler, R. and Harlowe, H.F. (1954). Curiosity in monkeys. *Scientific American,* 190, 70–75.

Cannon, W.B. (1932). *The Wisdom of the Body.* (Reprinted 1963.) New York: WW Norton.

Carroll, D. (1992). *Health Psychology: Stress, behaviour and disease.* London: The Falmer Press.

Caspi, A., Bolger, N. and Eckenrode, J. (1987). Linking person and context in the daily stress process. *Journal of Personality and Social Psychology,* 52, 184–195.

Cherry, E.C. (1953). Some experiments on the recognition of speech, with one and with two ears. *Journal of the Acoustical Society of America,* 25, 975–979.

Clements, A., Sharpe, M., Simkin, S., Borrill, J. and Hawton, K. (1997). Chronic fatigue syndrome: A qualitative investigation of patients' beliefs about the illness. *Journal of Psychosomatic Research,* 42, 615–624.

Cooper, C.L. and Marshall, J. (1978). *Understanding Executive Stress.* London: Macmillan.

Crombie, I.K. (1996). *A Pocket Guide to Critical Appraisal.* London: BMA .

Darwin, C. (1872). *The Expression of Emotions in Man and Animals.* (Reprinted 1965.) Chicago: University of Chicago Press.

Dawkins, R. (1976). *The Selfish Gene.* Oxford: Oxford University Press.

Ekman, P. (1994). All emotions are basic. In P. Ekman and R.J. Davidson (Eds) *The Nature of Emotion: Fundamental questions.* New York: Oxford University Press.

Empson, J. (1998). *Sleep and Dreaming.* Hemel Hempstead: Harvester Wheatsheaf.

Evans, P.D. and Edgerton, N. (1991). Life events and mood as predictors of the common cold. *British Journal of Medical Psychology,* 64, 35–44.

Eysenck, M. (1996). *Simply Psychology.* Hove: Psychology Press.

Fehr, B. and Russell, J.A. (1984). Concept of emotion viewed from a prototype perspective. *Journal of Experimental Psychology: General,* 113, 464–486.

Freud, S. (1914). *The psychopathology of everyday life.* New York: Macmillan.

Gaarder, J. (1995). *Sophie's World: A novel about the history of philosophy.* Translated Moller, P. London: Phoenix House.

Ganster, D.C. and Victor, B. (1988). The impact of social support on mental and physical health. *British Journal of Medical Psychology,* 61, 17–36.

Gatchel, R. (1997). Biofeedback. In A. Baum, S. Newman, J. Weinman, R. West, and C. McManus *Cambridge Handbook of Psychology, Health and Medicine.* Cambridge: Cambridge University Press.

Gleitman, H. (1991). *Psychology, 3rd edn.* London: WW Norton & Company.

Greer, S. and Morris, T. (1975). Psychological attributes of women who develop breast cancer: a controlled study. *Journal of Psychosomatic Research,* 19, 147–153.

Gross, R. (1996). *Psychology: The science of mind and behaviour.* London: Hodder & Stoughton.

Haynes, S.G., Feinleib, M. and Kannel, W.B. (1980). The relationship of psychosocial factors to coronary heart disease in the Framingham Study, III; eight year incidence of coronary heart disease. *American Journal of Epidemiology,* 3, 37–58.

Hebb, D.O. (1966). *A Textbook of Psychology.* Philadelphia: Saunders.

Horn, S. and Munafo, M. (1997). *Pain. Theory, research and intervention.* Buckingham: Open University Press.

Hull, C.L. (1943). *Principles of Behavior.* New York: Appleton-Century-Crofts.

Hygge, S. (1997). Noise: effects on health. In A. Baum, S. Newman, J. Weinman, R. West, and C. McManus *Cambridge Handbook of Psychology, Health and Medicine*. Cambridge: Cambridge University Press.

James, P. (1995). *Dermatology In Health Psychology: Processes and applications*, 2nd edn. Edited by Broome, A. and Llewelyn S. London: Chapman and Hall.

James, W. (1890). *Principles of Psychology*. New York: Henry Holt.

Kiecolt-Glaser, J.K., Garner, W., Speicher, C., Penn, G.M., Holliday, J. and Glaser, R. (1984). Psychosocial modifiers of immunocompetence in medical students. *Psychomatic Medicine*, 46, 7–14.

Kimble, D.P. (1988). *Biological Psychology*. London: Holt, Rinehart and Winston, Inc.

Kleinginna, P.R. Jr and Kleinginna, A.M. (1981). A categorized list of emotion definitions with suggestions for a consensual definition. *Motivation and Emotion*, 5, 345–379.

Kobasa, S.C., Maddi, S.R. and Kahn, S. (1982). Hardiness and Health: A prospective study. *Journal of Personality and Social Psychology*, 42,168–177.

Kop, W.J. and Krantz, D.S. (1997). Type A behaviour, hostility and coronary artery disease. In A. Baum, S. Newman, J. Weinman, R. West, and C. McManus *Cambridge Handbook of Psychology, Health and Medicine*. Cambridge: Cambridge University Press.

Lazarus, R. S. (1982). Thoughts on relations between emotions and cognitions. *American Psychologist*, 37, 1019–1024.

Lazarus, R.S. and Folkman, S. (1984). *Stress, Appraisal and Coping*. New York: Springer.

Levy, S. and Heiden, L. (1991). Depression, distress and immunity: risk factors for infectious diseases. *Stress Medicine*, 7, 45–51.

Linton, S. (1982). A critical review of behavioural treatments for chronic benign pain other than headache. *British Journal of Clinical Psychology*, 21, 321–327.

Lovallo, W.R. (1997). *Stress and Health: Biological and psychological interactions*. London: Sage.

Manning, A. and Dawkins, M.S. (1998). *An Introduction to Animal Behaviour*, 5th edn. Cambridge: Cambridge University Press.

Maslow, A.H. (1954). *Motivation and Personality*. New York: Harper and Row.

Mayer, J. (1955). Regulation of energy intake and the body weight: the glucostatic theory and the lipostatic hypothesis. *Annals of the New York Academy of Sciences*, 63, 15–43.

Miller, M.A. and Rahe, R.H. (1997). Life changes scaling for the 1990s. *Journal of Psychosomatic Research*, 43, 279–292.

McKinnon, W., Weisse, C.S., Reynolds, C.P., Bowles, C.A., and Baum, A. (1989). Chronic stress, leukocyte subpopulations and humoral response to latent viruses. *Health Psychology*, 8, 389–402.

Parkinson, B. (1995). *Ideas and Realities of Emotion*. London: Routledge.

Pennebaker, J.W. (1982). *The Psychology of Physical Symptoms*. New York: Springer-Verlag.

Prusiner, S.B., Scott, M.R., De Armond, S.J. and Cohen, F.E. (1998). Prion protein biology. *Cell*, 93, 337–348.

Rathus, S.A. and Nevid, J.S. (1989). *Psychology and the Challenges of Life*, 4th edn. London: Holt Rinehart and Winston.

Rosenmann, R.H., Brand, R.H., Jenkins, D., Friedman, M., Strauss, R, and Wurm, M. (1975). Coronary heart disease in the Western Collaborative Group Study: Final follow up experience of 8.5 years. *Journal of the American Medical Association*, 233, 875–877.

Sanders, D., Warner, P., Backstrom, T. and Bancroft, J. (1983). Mood sexuality, hormones and the menstrual cycle. *Psychosomatic Medicine*, 45, 487–501.

Schaeffer, M.A. and Baum, A. (1984). Adrenal corticol response to stress at Three Mile Island. *Psychosomatic Medicine*, 46, 227–237.

Schachter, S. and Singer, J. (1962). Cognitive, social and physiological determinants of emotional state. *Psychological Review*, 69, 379–399.

Selye, H. (1956). *The Stress of Life*. New York: McGraw Hill.

Slade, P. (1984). Pre-menstrual changes in normal women: fact or fiction? *Journal of Psychosomatic Research*, 28, 1–7.

Speisman, J.C., Lazarus, R., Mordkoff, A. and Davison, L. (1964). Experimental demonstration of stress based on ego-defense theory. *Journal of Abnormal and Social Psychology*, 68, 367–380.

Stellar, E. (1954). The physiology of emotion. *Psychological Review*, 61, 5–22.

Stone, A., Porter, L.S. and Neale, J.M. (1993). Daily events and mood prior to the onset of respiratory illness episodes: a non replication of the 3–5 day 'desirability dip'. *British Journal of Medical Psychology*, 66, 383–393.

Stratton, P. and Hayes, N. (1988). *A Student's Dictionary of Psychology*. London: Edward Arnold.

Sutherland, V.J. and Cooper, C.L. (1990). *Understanding Stress*. London: Chapman & Hall.

Thompson, J., Chung, M.C., Rosser, R. (1994). The *Marchioness* disaster: Preliminary report on psychological effects. *British Journal of Clinical Psychology*, 33, 75–77.

Tolman, E.C. (1948). Cognitive maps in rats and men. *Psychological Review*, 55, 189–208.

Weiner, B. (1986). *An Attributional Theory of Emotion and Motivation*. New York: Springer-Verlag.

Zajonc, R.B. (1984). On the primacy of affect. *American Psychologist*, 39, 117–129.

Zuckerman, M., Eysenck, S., and Eysenck, H.J. (1978). Sensation seeking in England and America: Cross cultural age, and sex comparisons. *Journal of Clinical and Consulting Psychology*, 46, 139–149.

GLOSSARY

Adrenal glands: Endocrine glands that secrete several hormones, such as cortisol, adrenaline (epinephrine), and nor adrenaline (norepinephrine), which are involved in stress reactions.

Adrenaline: Secretion of the adrenal medulla. Amongst its effects are raising of blood pressure, increasing the amount of glucose in the blood, and constricting the smaller blood vessels. Also known as epinephrine.

Antagonist: A drug that decreases or blocks the activity of a given neurotransmitter.

Anthropomorphic: Interpreting the actions of animals or physical objects as outcomes of processes similar to those of human beings.

Attribution: The process by which people attempt to judge or explain their own or others' behaviour.

Auto immune disease: A disease characterized by tissue injury caused by the immune system attacking the person's own tissue.

Buffering: The view that the health benefits of social support come from its reducing the negative health effects of high stress levels.

Circadian rhythm: Constant pattern of cyclical body activities that last approximately 24 hours and are determined by an internal 'biological clock'.

Cocktail party phenomenon: The phenomenon that one has to direct attention to one out of many possible simultaneous stimuli in order to make sense. For example, when you hear your name being mentioned in an otherwise noisy situtation.

Cognitions: Processes of knowing, including attending, remembering, and reasoning; also the content of these processes, such as concepts and memories.

Cognitive theory of emotion: A theory proposed by Schachter and Singer which asserts that emotions are an interpretation of our own autonomic arousal in the light of the situation to which we attribute it.

Common sense: As used in the discussion of artificial intelligence, the term refers to an understanding of what is relevant to a problem and what is not.

Conditioning: A term used to describe the process of learning.

Distress: A negative reaction to a stressor.

Double blind study: An experimental procedure whereby neither the subject nor the researcher knows which research treatment the subject is receiving.

Double depletion theory: A theory of thirst that water uptake of both cellular and extra cellular components influence water intake, and that these influences combine to produce the urge to drink.

Drive: An internal state of tension that guides us towards activities or objects that will reduce tension; provides the impetus for action.

Drive reduction theory: The theory that motivation occurs, and behaviour is energized, mainly or entirely as a result of the need to alleviate or reduce drives.

Dualism: Belief that the mechanistic body and brain act separately from the spiritual soul and ephemeral mind.

Emotions: The experience of subjective feelings which have positive or negative value for the individual.

Endocrine system: Glands that secrete hormones into the bloodstream.

Endogenous opioid peptides: Naturally-occurring morphine-like neurotransmitter in the brain, such as enkephalin. Important in pain perception.

Endorphins: Class of neurotransmitters involved in many reactions to pleasure and pain, literally, 'endogenous morphines'.

Eros: A term used by Freud to mean the driving force related to sexual urges and the preservation of the species.

Eustress: Positive reaction to a stressor defined as a challenge rather than a threat.

Free floating anxiety: Anxiety not focused on any particular agent or not associated with any known cause.

General Adaptation Syndrome (GAS): The sequence of physiological reactions to prolonged and intense stress. The sequence consists of the alarm reaction, the stage of resistance, and the stage of exhaustion.

Glucostatic theory of hunger: The idea that some index of glucose metabolism, such as blood levels, is critical in the regulation of food intake and body weight.

Homeostatic theory: The regulation of a constant internal physiological environment. Behaviours intimately related to homeostasis include feeding, drinking, and temperature regulation.

Humours: The Greeks (1500 BC) thought that ill health was due to an imbalance of humours: sanguine (yellow bile), choleric (blood), melancholic (black bile), and phlegmatic (phlegm).

Hypertonic: A solution that is more concentrated with respect to dissolved substances than the comparison solution. Often refers to a solution with more than 0.9 per cent concentration of Na^+ and Cl^- ions, the concentration in blood plasma.

Hypotonic: A solution that is less concentrated than a comparison solution. Often refers to a solution with less than 0.9 per cent concentration of Na^+ and Cl^- ions, the concentration in blood plasma.

Idealism: A view that only mental events are real.

Immune systems: The organs and structures that protect the body against harmful substances or agents, such as bacteria and viruses.

Incentive properties: The 'pull' exerted by a goal that motivates in the absence of need.

Interactionism: Behaviour that is jointly determined, either by personal *and* situational factors, or by mind *and* body.

Intuitive validity: When something appears to be correct in the absence of evidence.

Latent learning: Associations learned from experience and observation in which there is no change in behaviour at the time.

Leptin: A peptide produced in adipose tissue. It acts on leptin receptors in the hypothalamus to regulate energy balance.

Materialism: A view that only physical events are real.

Monism: View that mind and brain are aspects of a single reality.

Moods: Emotions that last for several minutes up to a few hours, where the subject is generally not concerned with how the feeling started.

Motivation: The general term given to an inferred underlying state which energizes behaviour, causing it to take place.

Neurotransmitter: A chemical involved in the transmission of impulses across the synapse from one neuron to another.

Non-organic illness: Illness with a physical origin.

Organic illness: Illness with no detectable physical origin.

Osmosis: When two solutions varying in concentration of some substance are separated by a membrane permeable to water, but not to the dissolved substance, water flows from the region of lesser concentration of the substance to the region of higher concentration. This movement of water is called osmosis.

Phase advance: Advancing the relationship between an endogenous rhythm and endogenous *zeitgebers*.

Phase delay: Delaying the relationship between an endogenous rhythm and endogenous *zeitgebers*.

Pineal gland: An unpaired organ in the brain whose functions in mammals are still poorly understood. Secretes melatonin.

Preganglionic sympathetic axons: Neurons that emerge from the spinal cord and then enter the sympathetic ganglia

Primary appraisal: The cognitive process people use in assessing the meaning of an event or situation for their well-being.

Primary motives: Motivational states that are induced by biological needs and not dependent on learning

Prion: An infectious agent, defined as 'a proteinaceous infectious particle which lacks neucleic acids' (Prusiner *et al.*, 1998). Examples of prion diseases include scrapie and CJD.

Prototype: Most representative example of a category.

Psychoimmunology: The study of relationships between psychosocial processes and endocrine, and immune system functioning.

Psychoneuroimmunology: The study of relationships between psychosocial processes and nervous, endocrine, and immune system functioning.

Psychophysiologists: Scientists interested in the relationship between the autonomic nervous system, behaviour, and emotion.

Reductionism: Belief that observable phenomena at one level of analysis can be accounted for by the working of phenomena at a more basic or fundamental level.

Secondary appraisal: The cognitive process people use in assessing the resources they have to meet demands.

Secondary motives: Motivational states that are dependent on learning.

Self-awareness: Sense of unified self.

Skinner Box: A small chamber in which there are a lever and a food dispenser in one wall. The rat learns to press the lever when pressing is reinforced by the delivery of a food pellet.

Stimulus: Environmental condition that elicits a response from an organism.

Strain: The psychological and physiological response to a stressor.

Stress: The condition that results when person/environment transactions lead the individual to perceive a discrepancy between the demand of a situation and his or her resources.

Stressors: Events or circumstances a person perceives as threatening or harmful.

Sympathetic Nervous System: A division of the autonomic nervous system that enables the body to mobilize and expend energy during emotional and physical arousal.

Thanatos: In Freudian theory, the death instinct, assumed to drive people toward aggressive and destructive behaviour.

Zeitgeber: An environmental event that captures or entrains a circadian rhythm.

ACKNOWLEDGEMENTS

Figure 2.1: Reproduced by kind permission of Professor Michael Argyle.

Figure 2.2: Janet Leigh from the film *Psycho*. © Paramount (courtesy The Kobal Collection, London).

Figures 2.3, 2.6, 3.2, 3.3, 4.1, 4.2, 4.3: Dr G.M. Alder.

Figure 3.1: Cartoon by Sanz from *Principles of Social Psychology* by Nicky Hayes, ©1993. Reprinted by kind permission of Psychology Press Limited, Hove, UK.

Figure 3.5: Reproduced by kind permission of the Harlow Primate Laboratory, University of Wisconsin.

Box 4.1: Based on *Journal of Psychosomatic Research*, 43, 279-292. Life changes scaling for the 1990s. M.A. Miller and R.H. Rahe, 1997, with permission from Elsevier Science.

ANSWERS TO SELF-ASSESSMENT QUESTIONS

SAQ1 The characters in a computer game appear to be human, but they are designed by programmers to set rules. They have no existence once the computer is switched off, and they are the product of the human mind, not of evolution. (You might have to explain Darwinian ideas of evolution too.)

SAQ2 The following are likely to be on your list: living organisms grow, reproduce, respond to stimuli, are made up of inorganic chemicals, contain DNA.

SAQ3 Early philosophers proposed that the non-physical mind is distinct from the physical brain. This has led to a separation of mind from body and made studying biopsychology difficult. The influence of dualism is still evident today in the labelling of illness as **organic illness** or **non-organic illness.**

SAQ4 No. The James–Lange theory does not explain either situation, and so is inadequate.

SAQ5

locus	internal – your own ability
stability	stable – can't change
controllability	uncontrollable – can't help it

Different attributions might make you feel even more motivated to improve your skills.

SAQ6 The interpretation (cognitive labelling) for point I might be that you are nervous of the task ahead, and for point 2 that you are about to have another heart attack.

SAQ7 A positive outcome might result from a secondary appraisal that considered looking forward to new challenges, anticipation of a redundancy financial package, a change of town or country, time to spend on travel, and a new social life. A negative outcome might be loss of social contact, financial hardship, loss of housing, or the effect on relationships.

SAQ8 When the body feels that it is being deprived of food, it switches to a more efficient use, so conserving weight rather than losing weight.

SAQ9 The common sense theory.

SAQ10 If you find studying stimulating, it is eustress. If you find that you get worried or anxious about studying, it might be distress.

SAQ 11 The elderly person would take longer to warm up. Their temperature regulation process is less responsive and they would feel the cold more than a younger person would.

SAQ12 The release of adrenaline would result in increased heart rate, increased blood pressure, sweating hands and pupil dilation. You might say that you felt alarm or fear (see *Figure* 2.4 in Part 2) increased heart rate, increased blood pressure, sweating hands and pupil dilation.

SAQ13 Phase delay.

SAQ14 They need to be in a constant state of arousal. If alerted there will be a rush of adrenaline resulting in an increase in heart rate, and glucose release from the liver and muscles.

SAQ15 Exercise, relaxation and seeking social support may all benefit health, and avoiding some of the behaviours discussed may prevent ill health.

SAQ16 It is not possible for the subject to be blind to the fact that they are relaxed. It may also be difficult for the experimenter to assess the person without noticing which group they are in. There may be a powerful placebo effect in the studies of the effect of relaxation.

SAQ17 A=2, B=3, C=4, D=1.

SAQ18 The problems should be identified. Is it the level of content? Then try discussing this with the tutor. Is it finding the time for study? You could make a timetable or reschedule other activities.

SAQ19 The beta-blockers, which probably act peripherally, rather than penetrating the brain, and block the activity of the sympathetic nervous system.

Lightning Source UK Ltd.
Milton Keynes UK
UKOW02f2153040414

229431UK00002BB/28/P